500 Questions and Answers

For New Teachers:

A Survival Guide

500 Questions and Answers

For New Teachers:

A Survival Guide

Joanna Montagna Torreano

Christopher-Gordon Publishers, Inc.

Copyright Acknowledgments

Every effort has been made to contact copyright holders for permission to reproduce borrowed material where necessary. We apologize for any oversights and would be happy to rectify them in future printings.

The Bill Harp Professional Teacher's Library

An Imprint of

Christopher-Gordon Publishers, Inc.

1502 Providence Highway, Suite 12

Norwood, MA 02062

800-934-8322

Printed in the United States of America

10 9 8 7 6 5 4 3 2 1   05 04 03 02 01 00

Library of Congress Catalog Card Number: 99-076804

ISBN: 1929024-09-6

Acknowledgements

To Lisa Brett LaBend, Patricia Seyfried Pearce, and Kristina Rice for reading my manuscript and making constructive suggestions for its improvement.

To Sue Canavan, executive vice-president at Christopher-Gordon Publishers, for accepting my manuscript in its infancy and believing in its merit. Thanks for helping my dream of publishing a book come true.

To all the first year teachers and education majors I've spoken with, thanks for sharing your thoughts with me.

To my husband, Paul, for his encouragement and support.

Dedication

This book is dedicated to all beginning teachers. ENJOY!!

Disclaimer

The questions included in this book are questions any beginning teacher may have. The degree to which you can implement my suggestions may vary from school system to school system.

My intent is to help you begin formulating possible solutions to everyday problems.

Table of Contents

Acknowledgements v

Dedication v

Introduction ix

Author's Credentials xi

Getting Your Act Together

What To Do Before School Opens 3

The First Day of School 9

Open House 15

Goal Setting 19

Last Day of School 23

Getting To Know You

Administrators 27

Board of Education 31

Parents 35

School Related Personnel (SRP) 41

Teacher's Union 45

Substitute Teacher 49

Getting to Know Your Students

Younger Children 55

Older Children: Grades 4-5 Transitioning to Grade 6 59

Ways of Learning 65

Special Education Students 69

How to Help Students Succeed

Writing and Spelling 77

Worksheets 87

Testing 91

Reading 95

Children's Books 105

Homework 107

Games 111

Field Trips 115

Computers 121

Family Suggestions 125

How To Keep Your Stress Down

Classroom Management 131

Discipline and All That Jazz 137

Time Management 143

Safety 145

Preparation and Lunch Period 149

Organizational Skills 151

Documentation 153

The Finals

Top Ten No-No's 161

Final Word—Top 10 Do's 163

Don't Give Up—It Gets Easier 165

Games Appendix 167

Reading and Writing References 171

Additional Suggested Readings 173

Introduction

This book is intended for anyone who is a beginning teacher. I have been teaching since 1975 and haven't forgotten what the first year of teaching felt like. I remember seeing *many* children lined up in front of my room and naively wondering what classroom they were going to be in. There were 36 children, dressed in uniform, ready to greet their teacher. Little did I know, I was their teacher. When they entered, the janitor had to bring three more desks. We were stuffed in a small classroom barely able to move.

I shut my door and wondered what I was going to do with them for 6 1/2 hours. The realization that all of those children were my responsibility was overwhelming.

Every day, I was going to quit. Every night I was going to quit. I made it through my first year with the help of caring teachers and a *wonderful* principal.

I *love* to teach now. My goal is to make your first year easier. I want to teach you tricks of the trade, and there are tricks.

The first suggestion I have for you is DON'T GIVE UP!! It does get easier. Every day I look forward to going in and teaching my children. When I started teaching, I looked forward to Saturday and Sunday. I would ask myself why I went to college for this? I made it through those first few years because I could count on support from my colleagues and principal. This book is intended to be your support.

Please read on to discover what you can do for yourself to nurture that joy of teaching.

First of all, give yourself permission to make mistakes! During your first year, you will make many mistakes. We all do. You are normal. You will go home upset over a child's home life. You are normal. You will come down hard on a child and feel bad about it. You are normal. You will feel insecure about yourself as a teacher. You are normal.

Teaching is a very isolating experience. You shut the door and you are on your own. This book will break the isolation. *Enjoy*, and keep teaching.

The format of this book is question and answer. I want to simplify the information as much as possible, since I know you may not have time to read every single page at one sitting. Read what you need and skip the rest.

In order to make this book a fast read, if a question is repeated in a previous chapter, I will ask you to refer to the page where it was noted first. There will be a "see page" reference.

Sit back and read the sections in any order. The only test will be how you interact with your students. Only you will know the results.

I have worked and continue to work with many beginning teachers. It is a relationship of mutual respect and trust. The only thing I keep telling new teachers—something I want to impress on you—whatever you are feeling you are *normal*!

Author's Credentials

Before you read this book, I think it is important for you to know who I am. I have a Bachelor's Degree in Elementary Education and a Master's Degree as a Reading Specialist, and have permanent New York State certification in both of these areas. I want you to understand that I know your fears, since I have lived through them myself. I also know your excitement because, after 24 years of teaching, I am still excited about my profession.

QUESTION:
Why did you write this book?

ANSWER:
In my present position as a reading specialist, I am fortunate to not only teach children, but also work with some wonderful beginning teachers. Since I am in and out of rooms all day, I have come to know their fears. I want to make your job easier and answer some of the questions I have been asked by beginning teachers. To continue growing as an educator, I have students who are studying to be teachers from a local university in my classroom on a regular basis. The questions they have posed to me are included in this book. In addition, I am on the staff at a local university where I teach a course to elementary majors.

QUESTION:
Have you always taught reading?

ANSWER:
No, I worked as a classroom teacher for four years. Two years in grade 3 and two years in grade 4. I have also worked as a math specialist, computer specialist, mentor teacher, and presently as a reading specialist. In my job as a computer specialist, I taught not only students in grades K–12, but also administrators, teachers and parents. Currently, in addition to my full time reading position, I am offering workshops to students preparing for a teaching degree at a local university.

QUESTION:
What did you learn as a classroom teacher?

ANSWER:
I learned that teaching is a very rewarding, yet demanding profession. With my present job as a reading specialist, my concentration is on reading. My children are taught using all modalities.

QUESTION:
Why did you leave the classroom?

ANSWER:
I wanted to be able to zero in on one specific area—reading. With my present background and experience I am able to teach children how to read through a variety of techniques. I now know if something doesn't work, I should try something else. I used to think if it didn't work, I did something wrong. Now I know that the particular technique I was using might not be best for that child. I learned that only through experience.

QUESTION:
What was your first year of teaching like?

ANSWER:
Confusing!!! I was apprehensive every step of the way. College prepared me with book

knowledge. Kids in the classroom were another whole dimension. Without the help of caring teachers and a wonderful principal, I wouldn't be doing what I love today . . . teaching.

QUESTION:
What did you learn as a mentor teacher?

ANSWER:
I learned that I knew a great deal about teaching, but most of that knowledge came from experience. There were some things you just had to live through. This book will help that "live through" experience be more enjoyable.

QUESTION:
If you had to pick a career today, what would you be doing?

ANSWER:
Teaching. I am a full-time reading specialist in an elementary building. I also present workshops to parents because I am interested in helping them help their children. My parent workshops are available to the 11 surrounding school districts through the local Board of Cooperative Educational Services (BOCES) In my spare time I co-produce and co-host an educational show at a local cable television station which is live, and airs every three weeks.

QUESTION:
What will I gain from reading this book?

ANSWER:
You will acquire needed information that you won't find in textbooks. You will also learn that no question is ever a "dumb" question. It is that unasked question that could put you in a lot of trouble.

QUESTION:
Is this book only for beginning elementary teachers?

ANSWER:
My knowledge base is elementary school—K-grade 5. I know my suggestions work with most of the children in that particular grade range. I'm not sure if all my ideas would work with older children. I've never had the opportunity to try them out on older students.

QUESTION:
Why aren't you mentoring now?

ANSWER:
Unfortunately, the mentor program wasn't funded. But I do help anyone who comes to my door. I also work with students at a local college who are planning on becoming teachers. After every lesson, we sit and talk about what I did and why I did it. I invite them to ask me any questions they want about a particular lesson. The college students also teach for me and I offer them suggestions when needed. It's a relationship of mutual respect. I love doing it.

QUESTION:
Any further plans?

ANSWER:
I enjoy writing and sharing what I have learned through my experiences. In addition, I want to keep growing as an educator. I subscribe to monthly educational journals. I feel it is important to keep current in my profession and continue to learn.

Getting Your

Act Together

What To Do
Before School Opens

There is a lot to be done before children walk in the door. You will have to go in several days beforehand to get things organized.

QUESTION:
When I walked into the room, everything was bare. How am I going to fill up all of those bulletin boards?

ANSWER:
The easiest way to fill up those bulletin boards is to use them over and over again for the same purpose. For example, let's suppose you use four bulletin boards. Use one bulletin board for *Helpers* of the week. Here you can cut out paper hands and have the children put their paper hand next to the chore they are doing. *Helpers* are needed to go to the office, pass out papers, water the plants, line leader, etc. You can change these *Helpers* weekly, but be consistent on the day. If you aren't consistent, the kids will drive you crazy wondering when the *Helper* chart is going to change. When children have been a helper, their name doesn't go up again until everyone has had a chance to help out. You can also use another bulletin board for *Good Work*. This can be very easily done by purchasing zip lock plastic bags where the good work is kept free from dirty hands. Each child has a zip lock bag to show good work. They love to see their work on display. It is a real motivator. You may want to use a third one for whatever content area you are covering. Perhaps for science, you are learning about plants. Here, you can put up information about plants. Maybe you are learning about contractions in reading. You can put up a bulletin board about contractions. The children will see this board often and it will reinforce what you are trying to teach. Using this method, you only have two that you need to change on a regular basis. The other two, "*Helpers*" and "*Good Work*" will stay the same throughout the year.

QUESTION:
I have 25 kids. Do I let them sit wherever they want, or do I assign seats?

ANSWER:
This is a very personal answer that is dependent on your teaching style. For myself, I like to give kids the benefit of the doubt. I like to let them sit with their friends provided they follow the rules. We'll get into rules later. If you let them sit where they want , you may want to provide each child with a half sheet of 8 1/2 x 10 paper on which they can write their name and decorate. This paper will go on the front of their desk *or* on top of

their desk to help you learn their names. They can decorate their paper with things they like to do. This gives you some idea of a child's interests. It is also helpful for a substitute or class visitors because it makes it easier for them to call a child by name.

QUESTION:
Should I have the children sit in rows or in pairs?

ANSWER:
This also depends on your style. I like to put children with someone else. In doing so, they have a buddy to sit, talk, and work with. Sometimes sitting with a buddy can get out of control. This is why you must have rules for classroom behavior and stick to the rules.

QUESTION:
What if I have an odd number of children? Where will this child sit?

ANSWER:
This is where you can get creative and have a threesome. Don't ever leave a child alone. Even if the child appears to be a loner, find a kind person to sit with this child to make this child feel comfortable.

QUESTION:
Where do I buy all the supplies I need for school? I need dictionaries, pencils, paper, etc.

ANSWER:
In some districts you are not responsible for buying any of your own material. Find out from a fellow teacher how supplies are ordered. I know in my building, for budgeting purposes we are asked around January to plan for the following year. Start thinking about the supplies you'll need for the first day of school . . . paper, pencils, chalk, glue, scissors. Also, before you order, check the room and see what is there. Someone was in that room before you were and usually there are all kinds of materials left behind. Also, some teachers will provide a list of supplies the first day of school that each child should purchase. You can mail this list to students prior to the beginning of school in a "Welcome to our Classroom Letter."

QUESTION:
My classroom doesn't have enough text books for everyone. I have 25 children and 23 books. What do I do?

ANSWER:
Talk to teachers who are teaching the same grade as you are. Perhaps someone has two books they are willing to let you borrow. If this doesn't work out, explain to your principal what you need. Sometimes books can be borrowed from another school in the same district. Make sure you check out the textbook situation before school opens.

QUESTION:
How do I find out about the discipline policy of the school?

ANSWER:
Make an appointment to talk with the principal before school opens. Ask what the policy is and how you should handle children who do not follow your policies. It is better to be prepared when it comes to handling difficult children.

QUESTION:
What about buses? How do I find out what buses the children go home on?

ANSWER:
Usually the secretaries at the office will have that information. On the first day of school, you get a packet which contains bus numbers for each child. If you would like this information before school begins, ask at the office. I suggest you get it before school opens, it is always better to be prepared.

QUESTION:
Why would I want bus information before the first day of school?

ANSWER:
You need to organize this information and compare it with the bus the child "thinks" s/he is going home on. You will be surprised at the number of mistakes you will find.

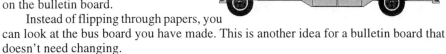

Imagine setting up a schedule for over 600 children—what a job! Some teachers like to cut out paper buses, put a child's name and bus number on them, and hang them on the bulletin board.

Instead of flipping through papers, you can look at the bus board you have made. This is another idea for a bulletin board that doesn't need changing.

QUESTION:
What about the planbook? Do I need to write in my plans for the first week?

ANSWER:
Yes, and *make sure* you write out the procedure for a fire drill and playground rules in your planbook and go over all of those procedures with the children. These rules should be available to you in a school handbook or ask at the school office. Should there ever be an accident involving a child, you need to prove that you have gone over the safety rules. In addition, the fire drill procedure needs to be placed on the wall by the exit door. If you have a substitute during a fire drill, the substitute will need this information.

QUESTION:
Is there such a thing as under planning for the first day of school?

ANSWER:
Yes, and if you under plan, you will be a nervous wreck! You need to *over* plan. For example, if you think an activity will take approximately 15 minutes, figure it will take 10. Calculate all the activities you will be doing and if it adds up to the total amount of hours in a school day, plan an extra activity in case you have miscalculated. You *need* to have things for kids to do. If you don't, they will find their own things to do.

QUESTION:
Should I put their names in the grade book before the start of school?

ANSWER:
I don't because your class list usually changes during the first few days of school. Children may get moved to another classroom or register late. I would have a list of my students and duplicate that list for the various subjects you want the list for. For example, you may want a separate list for reading, math, social studies, and science. You may also want a lunch list for students who buy lunch, get free lunch, or get reduced lunch. All you have to do is make one list and copy it. Once things have settled down, which is around the end of the first week, I put names in my grade book. When you print student names in your book, it's a good idea to skip every other line. Then, if you get a late addition, your book is still in alphabetical order.

QUESTION:
What else can I use the list for?

ANSWER:
The list could be used to record information such as the child's book number you are handing out for math or reading, etc. You may also want to keep track of who covers their books or who returns the note you sent home regarding needed school materials. You will want to keep that information somewhere and those copied lists will do the trick.

Sample Student List

Student Name	Rdg. Book	Math Book	Science Book	Soc. Book
Mary A.				
Joe B.				

Once you have made one list, duplicate it and change the headings.

QUESTION:
How do I find out what I have to teach?

ANSWER:
Each classroom should have a copy of state guidelines for each subject. If it doesn't, ask the office personnel where you can get a copy. Also, your school district should have guidelines as to what you need to cover. Ask at the Office for District Guidelines. If all of this fails, ask a colleague. Most of the textbooks that you will be teaching from already follow the state guidelines. That's how textbook companies sell books. They advertise the fact that their textbook meets state guidelines.

QUESTION:
Won't this take some time if I have to get guidelines mailed to me from the state?

ANSWER:
Yes, in the meantime, ask for the end of the year test. By browsing over the test, you will be able to see what is stressed in each subject area. I usually do it every year just as a refresher for myself. I was recently in a classroom where two teachers were sitting down and going over the end of the year test to analyze which items they needed to reinforce with their students.

QUESTION:
Can I show my students videos?

ANSWER:
School videos are safe to use. Videos that students bring from home MUST be rated "G", not "PG". You might want to check with your administrator or another teacher before showing any video that a student brings in. I know teachers show students videos right before a holiday break. It's an occasional treat that everyone enjoys.

QUESTION:
What can I do to introduce myself to my students before school opens?

ANSWER:
You might want to get names and addresses, and send a postcard to each child before opening day. Some teachers call their students a few days before school opens to say hello, and to tell the student how much they are looking forward to teaching them. This lessens the first day jitters for all and starts the year off with a positive tone.

QUESTION:
Is there any one item you would recommend purchasing?

ANSWER:
Yes, I mention this item throughout my book. I would recommend purchasing a date stamp. You can buy a date stamp at the grocery store. I date stamp the children's work and any notes that go home. I would also purchase a timer, nothing extravagant, just a timer you would use for baking. I use both of these items daily. Transitioning from activities is simpler when I set the timer. I can concentrate on teaching and not worry that the students have to go to the library in 40 minutes.

The First Day of School

The first day of school is very stressful for both the students and the teacher. There are many things that can and do go wrong. Be prepared and expect problems.

QUESTION:
I'm nervous. It's my first day on the job. I'm afraid I'll do something wrong. How can I calm myself down?

ANSWER:
Your feelings are very normal. I have been teaching for over 20 years and I still remember the first day jitters. In fact, every September brings on the first day jitters again. Be *prepared*. Be prepared to expect the unexpected. For example, expect tears if you are teaching younger children. Expect nervous parents—I know I was one of them when my son went to kindergarten. Expect bus problems. Children not knowing which bus to get on is very normal for the first week of school. Expect forgotten lunches. Expect new outfits from most of the children, but not from ALL of the children. Expect tired little kids at the end of the day. Expect that *you* will be tired by the time the children are ready to leave.

The first week of school is hectic for everyone. If you feel like you are on a merry-go-round that doesn't stop, your colleagues are feeling the same way. Things begin to settle down by the end of September.

If you need to come in early to get organized, do that. But don't stay too late after school—you could stay until midnight and everything wouldn't get done.

QUESTION:
How do I address parents? Do I call them by their first name?

ANSWER:
I always call my students' parents by their last names. But be careful, sometimes the child's last name is different from the parents. You need to be sensitive to last names. After a while, you may get to know some of the parents on a personal basis. You might want to call them by their first name, but I wouldn't start out that way.

QUESTION:
How do I assign lockers on the first day?

ANSWER:
It would be easier if you had all of their names on the locker the first day. A piece of masking tape with the child's first name and last initial will work. For safety reasons, it's best not to put a last name on a locker. Once you have established where a child's locker will be, you may want to use a permanent sticker instead of tape. You could

assign lockers alphabetically, or boy with boy, or boy with girl. Just be sure the name is clearly marked and spelled correctly. If you spell a name wrong, you can be sure the kids will tell you.

QUESTION:
What do I do if I can't get a child to stop crying?

ANSWER:
Unfortunately, there are some children that won't stop crying. I remember one little boy who clung to his mom and wouldn't let go. He had to be peeled off of her. It took about a week for the child to be all smiles when he entered the building.

Usually children will stop crying as soon as the parent leaves the room However, here are a few suggestions if the child doesn't stop crying . . . You can talk to the child and try to find out what his/her fears are. Usually the child will say, "I miss my mommy." You can reply, "Your mommy will be waiting for you when you get off the bus." You can try pairing the upset child with a child that seems to be having an easier time. You can also try ignoring the crying child. It may seem cruel to you, but sometimes a child will get better if there is no attention on the child. These suggestions don't always work, but they are a place to start. From my experience I know that eventually the crying does stop. Keep in mind this is a difficult time for both the parent and the child. My advice is to take it one day at a time.

QUESTION:
Should I let a parent take a child from my room at the end of the school day?

ANSWER:
You need to check out the procedure in your particular building. I know that where I teach *all* parents must report to the office and children are dismissed from the office. The reason for this is that there are many children who are not allowed to see one parent. To avoid the "legal problems" of families, children are *all* dismissed from the office.

QUESTION:
How do I help my students get to know each other? What kinds of activities can I plan?

ANSWER:
I saw an interesting activity that I'll pass on to you.

There were 10 questions that went like this: Find someone who has one brother; Find someone who hates pizza; Find someone whose first name begins with the same letter of your first name; etc. Doing this activity breathes life into your students. (Sometimes too much life!) As the teacher, you can choose to be a part of this activity or be an observer. The important part is to watch and see how the children interact with one another. After a certain period of time, you can have the children sit in a circle and share what they found out about each other. This is a great icebreaker and can generate conversation later.

QUESTION:
I have a lot of board games I want to teach my children to play. I'm not sure they'll be ready for all of them on the first day. How should I introduce the games?

ANSWER:
Introduce the games very slowly. Just show them one or two games at a time. Explain the directions fully so they won't bother you when you are trying to teach other children. Also, it may be a good idea to have one child be the "teacher" for that game. If the kids have any questions, they can go and ask that particular child. By showing the kids a few games at a time, you will always have a new game to show them which will keep their interest peaked.

QUESTION:
How do I get everyone going the first day? What do I teach?

ANSWER:
You will spend most of your day teaching classroom rules. However, you need to break up the listening by doing things. Children, as well as adults, cannot listen all day. For example, model how children are to walk in the halls. To do this, take them for a walk and get them moving. When you come back in the classroom, talk about their behavior and what you liked and what you didn't like. Talk about the lunch procedure. Model for them what is acceptable in your classroom as far as lining up, getting their lunches, where children stand who are buying, where children stand who have brought a lunch. You will also need to model what your expectations are during a fire drill. How can you do this? Pretend there is a fire drill, and take them to the exact spot they are required to go. To break up the day, play a few games of Simon Says, Mum Ball, or Four Corners. (See Games Appendix for explanation of games.) Go over rules regarding what to do when a visitor is in the room. Do you expect your children to say hello to a visitor? If so, have a child pretend s/he is a visitor and have the children greet this person with a smile and a hello. What about notes they bring to you first thing in the morning? Show the children where you expect all notes to go. Do you want them on your desk in a box marked "Notes"? Show them. You will spend most of your first day modeling appropriate behaviors. It is *not* a waste of time. The first few days set the tone for the rest of the school year. You may not be teaching academics, but you will make the teaching of academics easier when children know behavioral expectations. I recently spoke with a first year teacher who is just completing six months of his first year. I asked him what he would have done differently. He told me he wished he had stressed the rules of his class. He said once patterns of bad behavior were established, they were hard to break.

QUESTION:
Where else can I go to keep kids moving?

ANSWER:
Some of your students may be new to the school. This is a great time to show everyone where you find the office, library, gym, and nurse. I am forever finding kids wandering around the halls that first week of school looking for a specific place. Once they find it, they don't know how to get back to their own classroom. Model this for the kids and take them out for a walk.

QUESTION:
You mentioned fire drills. What about children who are at speech or reading class during a fire drill?

ANSWER:
Those children will walk out of the room with the speech or reading teacher. They will be accompanied by that teacher to the spot where their classroom teacher is with the rest of the children. Remember, as the classroom teacher, you must know where your children are at all times. If a fire bell rings, and the children are unsupervised in the halls walking back to a room, they *need to be told* to exit out of the first door they see and meet you at the designated spot. They will know this spot since you modeled it for them the first day of school. I have asked my kids what they would do if the fire bell rang and they were in the hall on the way to my room. They responded, "Oh, I'd go and look for my teacher". I have then taken them in the hall and modeled what they should do. Most children say, "Oh, I never knew I should go out the nearest door. "

QUESTION:
Once the rules are made, what next?

ANSWER:

It is usually fun to have the children tell you something special they did over the summer. I remember doing that as a kid in school and it still works. You can have them discuss this in a group or whole class. After discussing their experiences, they can draw a picture and write about it. Date this paper with the date stamp you purchased at the grocery store. You will want to show them at the end of the year how much they have grown. At the end of the year, you can ask them to draw what they plan to do for the summer and write about it. Then compare the two papers to see the growth. Don't worry about their spelling, just let them express themselves the best way they can. You'll learn a lot about them if the writing is spontaneous.

QUESTION:

It seems like I'm wasting a lot of time going over class rules the first day. Is this necessary?

ANSWER:

You will never regret the fact that you have established rules and consequences. If you don't, you will soon have chaos. There will be little learning going on in your room. My first year was chaotic until November because I didn't set up rules and consequences. I thought everyone would obey because that's the way it should be. Was I ever wrong. Kids are kids. They will try to see what they can get away with. Let them know from the first day that your room is a place to have fun *and* learn.

QUESTION:

It takes a long time to go over the rules. What do I do after that?

ANSWER:

If you model all the procedures, it will take you quite a bit of time. Remember children are not only listening to your expectations, they are also doing them. Get them moving. Line them up, walk them around. In addition, you will have books to pass out, seating arrangements to make, a note with needed school supplies for parents, a book to read to them, time for them to relax with a book on a rug (if you're lucky enough to have a rug),and a get acquainted activity. Also, build in time for the children to sit and draw or color with soft music in the background. Hopefully, you will have a tape recorder in your room. If not, find out where you can borrow one. After lunch is a great time to have children listen to soft instrumental music and draw. My first principal suggested this calming down strategy to me as a first year teacher. She was right. It calmed everyone down, including me. Finally, leave yourself some time at the end of the day to go over end of the day routines such as getting things out of the locker, packing up the backpack, putting on sweaters or boots, lining up for dismissal, and bus calling procedure.

QUESTION:

Isn't that a lot of talking? Will they remember all the rules?

ANSWER:

No, they won't. That's why you go over the rules again on day two, day three and day four. Do this until it becomes second nature for all the kids. You should also keep reinforcing your rules throughout the school year, especially when you have returned from a holiday.

QUESTION:

How do I get their attention when they are all talking at once?

ANSWER:

I have used several different techniques. Since most children are on their best behavior the first day of school, make sure you cover how you want them to behave when you need their attention.

Suggestion #1   You can always dim the lights and tell children you expect them to freeze where they are and look at you for further directions. This method works for all grades.

Suggestion #2   I saw this second method used by a student teacher. She very quietly said "Chocolate" and the children answered "Chip." After they said "Chip" all mouths were closed and they were told to look at the teacher.

Suggestion #3   I saw this method in a classroom of a first year teacher. She rings a bell. Everyone has been taught to stop what they are doing when they hear the bell. She then waits for the talking to stop and says, "Stop" (puts her hand out in front of her) "Look" (puts her hand to her eyes) and "Listen" (puts her hand to her ears) The children chant with her, "Stop, Look and Listen." It works every time.

Yes, there are children who do not adhere to any of the above methods. That is where consequences for inappropriate behavior come into play.

QUESTION:
How do I let them know how much noise is acceptable?

ANSWER:
Model it. For instance, I saw a school that had levels of noise that were posted. It looked something like. this:

      Level 0   No noise
      Level 1   Whispering Only
      Level 2   Inside voices
      Level 3   Outside voices

If you want to model Level 0, ask everyone to be quiet. Tell them that is what Level 0 should sound like. Then ask everyone to whisper to the person next to them. Tell them that is Level 1. Do all the levels that way. Then make a game out of it, ask the kids to show you Level 2. Wait a few minutes and tell them.to show you Level 0. This is a good tool to use. While teaching, you may tell your kids you need Level 2 voices, not Level 3. They will all know what you mean. Kids are kids, they will try to see what they can get away with. Teach them the rules and expect them to be followed.

QUESTION:
What about bathroom privileges and getting drinks of water? How do I handle that?

ANSWER:
Some classrooms have bathrooms right in the room. Make a "Stop and Go" sign that can be hung on the door handle. Model for children what should be done with the signs. It may sound silly but model, model, model and you'll never go wrong. I'd advise telling children they can use the bathroom whenever they need to, however, they should try and *not* go while you are teaching. Of course, there will be "emergencies" and children should be able to use the bathroom. If the bathroom is not in your room, set up a procedure. Have the children write their name on the board under "Bathroom Privileges". If they are older students, have them write the time they left and the time they return. Reason? If there are problems in the bathroom, you can locate the suspect much quicker. Do you want the children to take water breaks throughout the day or do you want a scheduled break? You can write "Water Privileges" on the board and have children sign in and out for them too.

     My first year of teaching, I told my principal I wanted my children to be independent and not ask me for water. I wanted my students to have water available at all times. I didn't have a fountain in my room so a child brought in a large jug which we filled with water. I told the children they could get water anytime they wanted with their individual plastic cups. You guessed it— not only did they drink water all day, but they also needed to use the bathroom. That jug went home the very same day, never to be seen again. My principal chuckled as she saw the jug leave. She said, "Joanna, I knew it wouldn't work, but you had to find it out for yourself. You'd always resent me if I told you not to have the jug. You had to learn for yourself." Whenever I see my first principal, we chuckle about the water incident.

QUESTION:
Should I start teaching science and social studies the first day of school?

ANSWER:
Once students know your expectations, teaching comes easily. Don't worry about social studies and science the first day. Concentrate on the routines that have been described.

QUESTION:
There are certain supplies I'd like my children to have. Can I send home a list of re-quested items?

ANSWER:
Yes, but before you send a note home, check out the school policy for notes that are sent home to parents. Some schools require all notes to be pre-approved by an admin-istrator. Other schools are not as strict. Ask a veteran teacher about school-supplied materials. I remember I asked the children to bring in crayons and afterwards, my administrator told me a box of crayons was supplied for each child. So check it out before you send the note home. Some suggestions of needed supplies are pencils, eras-ers, glue, markers, etc.

QUESTION:
Once the children come off the bus and are in the room, how do I occupy the time before everyone arrives?

ANSWER:
Have something on the chalkboard they must read and do each morning. Perhaps you want them to sit and talk to one another. You could write:

Aa Bb Cc Dd Ee Ff Gg Hh Ii Jj Kk Ll Mm Nn Oo Pp Qq Rr Ss Tt Uu Vv Ww Xx Yy Zz

Good Morning

Please take your seat and tell the person next to you what you did last night that you enjoyed.

Be ready to share this with the class.

Are your pencils sharpened?

Open House

At the beginning of the school year, most schools hold an Open House. The Open House is usually scheduled during the evening hours so that working parents can attend. Some schools welcome children during open house. Some schools prefer children stay at home, which gives the teacher the ability to talk about classroom policies.

QUESTION
What is an Open House?

ANSWER
An Open House is when parents are invited to the school to meet the teachers and principal.

QUESTION
What do I talk about during an Open House?

ANSWER
That depends, let me give you two different scenarios. Let's suppose children are allowed. You could do the following. Outside your doorway, have a desk with copies of the following paper. Also have a sign in sheet, so you can refer back to who came that evening.

Open House

Welcome to Open House. Enjoy your visit. Ask your child, to please do the following:

1. Show your parents where your desk is.
2. Show your parents all the textbooks.
3. Show your parents the chart on the wall that has our daily specials.
4. Introduce me to your parents.
5. Show your parents the gym, library, and nurse's office.
6. Take your parents to the cafeteria to enjoy some refreshments.

The items included may be changed to meet your particular needs. Also, I would recommend changing the order of the items.

Open House

1. Introduce me to your parents.
2. Show your parents the gym, library and office.
3. Show your parents where your desk is.

In doing so, you won't have 25 parents waiting to be introduced to you.

QUESTION
What if children are not allowed? How is Open House different?

ANSWER
Without children, it is easier to hold small meetings with parents. In one school, parents have 15 minutes with a particular teacher. Then a bell sounds and parents move on to the next classroom. Remember most parents have to visit more than one teacher during Open House. While parents are with you, you can explain your classroom rules and methods of discipline. You can show them the required texts. You may want to explain your grading policy. Let them know the school phone number for the times they want to get in touch with you. Encourage parents to call you if something is going on at home that may be affecting their child's learning. Also have a sheet for parent conferences available where parents can put in times they would be available. This saves a lot of hassle before parent conference time.

Parent Conference Sheet

Please sign up for a time that is convenient for you.
I will get back to you to confirm the day and time.

Monday Sept. 7, 7:00 PM _____

Monday Sept. 7, 7:15 PM _____

Monday Sept. 7, 7:30 PM _____

Monday Sept. 7, 7:45 PM _____

QUESTION
Couldn't I have a parent conference at Open House?

ANSWER
Usually Open House is scheduled at the beginning of the school year. It is better NOT to discuss a child's progress at this time. Reason? You need time to formulate an opinion about this child. When notices go home informing parents about Open House, you may want to state that the meeting is a general meeting. You would prefer NOT to discuss individual children. Most parents will honor your request. However, some won't.

QUESTION
What do I do if a parent wants to know a child's individual progress?

ANSWER

Just tell them it is too early in the school year to give an honest evaluation of their child. Explain how you are getting to know all 25 of your students. If this child is a discipline problem, go ahead and tell the parent.

QUESTION

How long does Open House last?

ANSWER

Each district handles this differently. Generally Open House lasts about an hour and a half. That is long enough after teaching all day.

Goal Setting

When you realize all that has to be taught in a school year, it can be overwhelming. You need to pace your teaching for an entire year. You need to set your own goals.

QUESTION:
How am I supposed to know what I am required to teach?

ANSWER:
You should have a curriculum guide for all subject areas that explains what is expected of you as a teacher. The curriculum guide will explain what needs to be taught for that particular year. If the room you are in doesn't have a current guide, ask your administrator or another teacher. Or, write to the state education department to get a current copy of the curriculum guide.

QUESTION:
Now that I know what I am to teach, how much time do I give to each academic area?

ANSWER:
This is where preplanning is important. Make yourself a graph and list the months your school is in attendance. Under each month write down what you hope to cover in each subject area. Pace yourself for the entire year and try to reach that goal. You may want to fill out a sheet of paper for each subject area. During your planning, keep in mind that near the end of the year, you will need to give yourself time for test preparation. Test preparation usually begins about a month before the standardized test. There are concepts that must be taught *before* the end of the year so the children will have a fair chance at the test.

Sample Math Curriculum Plan for the School Year											
Math Curriculum											
Sept.	Oct.	Nov.	Dec.	Jan.	Feb.	Mar.	Apr.	May	June	July	Aug.
Go over facts from last	Teach simple (+) and (-) facts	Teach simple (x) facts.					Pre pare for end of the year test.		Give end of the year test.		

This is just a brief sample. I haven't filled in all of the months. Using this simple graph will help you figure out just how much time you can spend on a concept.

QUESTION:
How do I pace the school day?

ANSWER:
You will have to sit down and figure out just how much teaching time you really have. Keep in mind there is lunch, and usually a daily special. A daily special would be gym, art, music, etc. After you have calculated all of the specials, and the morning and after-noon announcements, you'll know how much time you have to teach. I also recommend that you leave time at the end of the day for the end of the day duties such as homework, announcements, and any reminders that you need to give the children.

For example, let's take a look at a typical school day:

Morning announcements	15 minutes
Special class, i.e. gym, library	35 minutes
Lunch	30 minutes
	10 minutes to walk to and from
Bathroom/Water break	15 minutes
End of the day activities	15 minutes
Total time	120 minutes

Let's suppose your total day is 7 hours, or 420 minutes. 120 minutes of that time is used for non-academic lessons. This leaves you with approximately 300 minutes of teaching time, or 5 hours. This is a big difference from the 7 hours you may have thought you had.

QUESTION:
Parents have told me that when they ask their kids what they learned in school, the answer is "Nothin." Is there a way to teach my kids to give an appropriate answer?

ANSWER:
At the end of the day, make it a ritual to ask the children what they learned today in reading, math, social studies, etc. Have them be very specific. Then model for them a conversation they may have at home. For example, you can ask someone, "What did you learn in school today?" They might reply, "I learned in social studies that the state

I live in is New York and the city I live in is Niagara Falls. " The answer should now be specific instead of just plain "nothin." Make this a part of your closure for the day. Each day you could have a different child be the parent and another child model an appropriate answer.

QUESTION:
The science and social studies books have a lot of material. Am I expected to teach all of it?

ANSWER:
You will need to look at your curriculum guide to determine what is expected in your grade. Make sure you cover all of the expected material. If you have time left over, you can discuss the other chapters.

QUESTION:
I feel as if I'll never get through everything that is required. How do I set priorities?

ANSWER:
Talk to a colleague in the same grade level. Find out the most important areas to teach and make sure you teach those areas. Also, look at the end of the year tests. This will give you a reasonable idea of what areas will need to be taught.

QUESTION:
What end of the year tests?

ANSWER:
Most schools give standardized, end of the year tests that children are required to take. In New York state, there are several regents exams students must pass before they get a regents diploma. In addition, younger children have state-wide tests administered to them beginning in 4th grade. Find out the requirements in your state from a colleague.

QUESTION:
Where do I get this test?

ANSWER:
It isn't just one test. There are tests for reading, math, social studies, etc. Ask a colleague to show you a sample test from prior years. Some schools don't give the end of the year tests, but most do.

QUESTION:
Are standardized tests and standards the same thing?

ANSWER:
No, standardized tests are normed throughout the United States. However, when standards are developed, standardized tests are on the mind of those developing the standards.

QUESTION:
What are standards?

ANSWER:
Standards are state-wide, agreed upon expectations that all children will meet. For example, there may be a standard that all children will read and comprehend the written word at a second grade level by the end of second grade. That is a standard for second grade in some states. Depending on the school, a standardized test may be administered to determine whether or not a child has met not only the state-wide standard, but also the national standard.

QUESTION:
What are benchmarks?

ANSWER:
Benchmarks are small steps a person has to reach before they meet the standard. For example, a kindergarten teacher may have the benchmark of teaching students the alphabet and the sounds of the letters. That benchmark is needed for the child to reach the first grade standard of being able to read.

QUESTION:
Who decides the standards?

ANSWER:
Generally, a committee consisting of teachers and administrators decide the standards and benchmarks for each grade.

QUESTION:
Do all states have standards?

ANSWER:
As of this writing, 48 states have adopted content standards in reading/language arts and math. The standards are grouped by grade. The groups are grades 3-5, 6-9, and 10-12.

Last Day of School

Before you know it, you will be looking at the last day of school. The school year always seems to fly by. There are necessary steps that need to be taken before you close the door. Below are a few of them.

QUESTION:
Teachers have told me I have to put test stickers on a student's permanent record card. What is a permanent record card and what are test stickers?

ANSWER:
The permanent record card is a card that is usually kept in the school office. This card has a child's standardized test scores from kindergarten through graduation from high school . Test stickers are test results from standardized tests that come in the form of a sticker. They are placed on the permanent record card at the end of the year.

QUESTION:
What is the purpose of the permanent record card?

ANSWER:
It is a way of keeping track of a child's progress. Also, if a parent requests to see this card, you may show them.

QUESTION:
Can I take the permanent record card to my room to read it over carefully?

ANSWER:
In my building, you have to sign for it from the office. Once you have signed the card out, you may take it to your room. However, it should *not* leave the building. It is the permanent record of a child. If it ever got lost, it would be a problem.

QUESTION:
Is the permanent record card the same as the permanent record folder?

ANSWER:
No. The folder may contain letters from parents that were written to teachers . This folder can also contain documentation that parents refused retention, or remedial or special educational services. If a students has been troublesome on the bus, the bus note is in this folder. At the end of each school year, 40 week report cards are placed in

the folder. This folder should not leave the building. The permanent record card contains test scores from all standardized tests.

QUESTION:
The principal has asked me to put my students in categories according to grade average. Why?

ANSWER:
Usually, administrators like to academically balance a class. If your principal is asking you to do this, it's because your next class will have some A students, B students, C students, etc.

QUESTION:
I'm repeating a child. Can I request to have that child for the next school year?

ANSWER:
If you feel it is in the best interest of the child and you have parent support, go ahead and ask your principal.

QUESTION:
Parents have asked me which teacher their child should get for the next school year? What do I do?

ANSWER:
I would recommend *never* pitting one teacher against another. I'm asked this question frequently. I tell parents all teachers have their strong and weak points, including me. I invite them to ask other parents.

QUESTION:
Can I have an end of the year party?

ANSWER:
Sure!

QUESTION:
Why do I have to pack everything up at the end of the year?

ANSWER:
Some schools require this and others don't. If you are asked to pack, it is usually because your room may be changed to another part of the building. It is a nuisance, but it is easier to pack things yourself. Label the contents outside the box so you'll be able to quickly locate your materials when you return from the summer vacation.

QUESTION:
I feel very sad that my first class is leaving me. Any helpful hints?

ANSWER:
Not really. I can still remember my first class even without looking at their names on the school picture. Your first class will always be close to your heart because you grew and learned together. You won't forget them. If you want a special memory of your class, you might want to buy fabric crayons and have each child draw a picture on a plain white sheet of paper. After they are finished drawing, iron on their fabric drawn pictures to a canvas bag or sweatshirt. This way, you'll always have a memory of your class. Be careful not to have any letters or numbers on the drawing, since everything comes out backwards.

On the last day of school, I go to the bus circle to wave good-bye to the children. There are a few teachers who join me. It's an end of the year ritual. Start it, you'll enjoy it.

Getting To

Know You

Administrators

Administrators are the "administers" of the building. They are responsible for what goes on in the building. As often as possible, keep your administrator appraised of your classroom activities and any problems that may arise. They cannot help you if they don't know about a problem.

QUESTION:
This is my first year and my administrator is always in my room asking me questions while I'm teaching. What can I do about this?

ANSWER:
Well, the easiest thing to do is to talk to your principal after school and ask why s/he is in your room while you are teaching. This has to be done tactfully. Explain why it bothers you and ask if s/he could come in only occasionally. If you don't want to do this, you may want to go to a trusted colleague and see if s/he has any ideas for you. My first year of teaching was difficult, but I had a wonderful principal who was extremely supportive. However, I was still nervous when she walked by my room. I always thought she was watching me. She may have been, or may not have been. As a first year teacher, you are insecure. Most administrators are not out to get you, they do want to help. Find out why your principal keeps coming in.

QUESTION:
My administrator doesn't like the way I write my lesson planbook. I was never taught in college how to keep a planbook . What do I do?

ANSWER:
Find a colleague who you can talk with and ask to see his/her planbook. This will help you quickly figure out what you are doing wrong.

A Sample Planbook Entry

Monday   Obj. To teach addition of single digits up to 6

            Method: Using manipulatives, students will put 3 items on their desk and then put 2 more. They will then add then together. We will do several of these before we move to paper and pencil.

            Book: (Name of series), page 4, Problems 1-5 together, 6-10 on own for evaluation purposes.

Notice the objective, materials, and the evaluation are all clearly stated. Most administrators want this information.

QUESTION:

I'm having trouble with a parent. Should I tell my administrator, or handle it myself?

ANSWER:

"How can I help you if I don't know you are having a problem?" a principal once asked me. This is very true. Now, if I see a potential problem with a parent, I will go to the principal and explain my version of the story *before* the parent explains their version. In doing this, the principal has a better handle on what is going on. Sometimes, parents have been told their version by their child, and it may be different from your perspective. This allows the principal to get the facts quicker. Don't go for small annoyances, just for the biggies. Talk to colleagues about what you should tell your principal. You don't want to go for every little thing. As a first year teacher, you should find someone who can help you know the difference.

QUESTION:

I like my principal, but most people dislike him. I'm uncomfortable when the talk turns to him. What do I do?

ANSWER:

Keep quiet. Your silence speaks many words. You don't have to chime in with the rest of the people. Good for you that you can see something good about your administrator.

QUESTION:

I want to repeat a child, but my administrator doesn't believe in retention. What do I do?

ANSWER:

If the parent and administrator are *both* against retention, you're fighting a losing battle. Document in the child's folder that you feel the child will have a difficult time in the next grade if the child is not repeated. Instead of "Promoted to Grade 4", you might cross out promoted and write "Placed."

I have heard parents say to me, "I never knew John was having a hard time. No one ever told me." When I check back and read the folder, I can see which teacher did inform the parent. Keep accurate records of all your students.

If your administrator is against retention, but the parent *wants* retention, suggest that the parent go and talk to the administrator. There are very few administrators that will go against a parent's wishes . You can prepare the parent by giving them papers that the child has done incorrectly. There has been a strong movement against retention, but recently there has been an equally strong movement to higher standards for all children. Some educators realize that social promotion has got to stop. Personally, I think if a child doesn't understand something that needs to be built on in the next grade, we are only promoting frustration. That is my opinion and is not equally shared by all. I have repeated children and have never regretted that decision. It's not an easy decision to make, but you have to think about the child at all times. Ask yourself, what is best for this child?

QUESTION:
My principal believes in retention. Is there a procedure I should follow before I talk to the parents of a student I am thinking of repeating?

ANSWER:
Yes, you should always let your principal know who you are planning on repeating. Not only is it courteous to do so, but it also avoids a potential problem. A parent may refuse retention and talk to the principal without your knowledge. If you have already discussed the situation with the principal, you are in the clear. It is also wise to let your principal know the reasons for retention. Remember the administrator is responsible for all that goes on in the building. Keep him/her informed.

QUESTION:
I'm the new kid on the block and my administrator expects me to stay for many after school functions. I don't want to stay. What do I do?

ANSWER:
Pick and choose the ones you can stay for and explain why you can't stay for all the functions. If you are a first year teacher, administrators will be evaluating you. However, you do have a life after school, so pick and choose those activities you can participate in.

QUESTION:
I love to hang decorations on my door and my administrator told me to take them down, but didn't give me an explanation. Do you know why?

ANSWER:
Unfortunately, we live in a society where children can be abused not just by people they don't know, but by people they know. Keeping your door clear so people can look in at all times protects *you* from being accused of any wrongdoing. I also teach with my door open so anyone can walk in. It's just my philosophy.

QUESTION:
It's my first observation by my principal. Any suggestions?

ANSWER:
Yes, keep your objective simple. Don't try to do something fancy. Present the lesson as you normally would. If you try and teach differently, your children will react differently. The most important areas your principal will be looking at are the behavior of your students and whether or not you are meeting the needs of *all* your children.

QUESTION:
Is there a simple way to monitor childrens' behavior?

ANSWER:
Yes, watch where you stand. If you are pointing to something at the chalkboard, where is your back? Are you blocking some children's view? If so, the children can't see what you are trying to explain and you can't see what they are doing. You have to almost paste your back to the front of the chalkboard. Always move around when teaching. If you stay in one spot, you are inviting trouble. If you move around a lot, children will

never know where you will end up. This keeps everyone on their best behavior.

QUESTION:
When will I ever feel like I'm an adequate teacher? Even after a positive evaluation, I still get nervous.

ANSWER:
A little nervousness is a good thing, I think it keeps us on our toes. Right now, I'm at the stage in my life where I care more and more about how I teach and I don't care as much about my evaluation. The person that is the hardest on me is me. The more confident you become as a professional, the more you 'll realize that there is always something to learn. An administrator is *a* person looking at you periodically. The person who looks at you daily is *you*.

QUESTION:
My principal evaluated me and was supposed to give me that evaluation in writing after five days. I haven't seen it yet, what do I do?

ANSWER:
Administrators are very busy people. Perhaps it was just an oversight. The next time you see your administrator, ask to see your evaluation. Mention that you know schedules are busy, but suggest some possible meeting times.

QUESTION:
I don't like my administrator. Our philosophies are not the same. Jobs are hard to come by, what do I do?

ANSWER:
Working for someone who shares a different educational philosophy than you can be difficult. To survive, stay as far away from this person as possible. Say very little so you won't be accused of going against your administrator's philosophy. Find teachers who support your philosophy and share with them. Administrators come and go, teachers usually hang around. Keep the faith, someone good may be coming down the pike.

QUESTION:
My principal stays in the office and I don't really know him/her. I'm very uncomfortable when I have to talk to him/her. What should I do?

ANSWER:
Well, there isn't much you can do. Some people administer from afar. Just do your job and when you need to ask him/her something, go in knowing that you will get an answer but no warm fuzzies.

QUESTION:
My administrator wants me to present a workshop for other teachers and I'm uncomfortable about that. What do I do?

ANSWER:
Identify your "uncomfortableness". Do you know the material? Are you afraid of making a mistake in front of your colleagues? Do you just not want to give the workshop? Figure out *why* you don't want to give the workshop and then go and talk to your administrator. I had an administrator who kept throwing workshop ideas on my desk. I kept throwing them in the garbage. One day he asked me why I didn't want to conduct workshops and I told him I was afraid. He told me he knew I could do it. I did, and I have been doing them ever since. My "uncomfortableness" was a fear of teaching teachers. Teachers can be critical, but they are also wonderful caring people who want to learn. So, figure out what your fear is and do what is best for you.

Board of Education

School districts are divided into geographical areas. Each district has its own governing body called the Board of Education (BOE) The Board of Education members are elected residents of the district. The practices and procedures mentioned below might vary from state to state.

QUESTION:
Who is my boss? Is it my principal or the Board of Education?

ANSWER:
Actually, you have an immediate boss, which would be the principal, and a group of people (Board of Education) who are not only your boss, but the principal's boss as well.

QUESTION:
Who are the Board of Education?

ANSWER:
They are a group of people elected by the residents of a school district. They oversee the running of the school and make policies.

QUESTION:
What type of credentials do you have to have to be on the Board of Education?

ANSWER:
Generally, an interest in education would be the priority. You do *not* have to have a degree in education or a degree in any subject matter. Most districts require that you express an interest in writing to be a member of the board. You would need to run for office and be elected by the residents of your school district.

QUESTION:
How do board members get the residents approval?

ANSWER:
The people who run for the Board of Education go to the residents to determine what is wanted for their schools. They can then make a platform based on needs and desires of the district residents. They base their campaign on issues relevant to the district citizens.

QUESTION:
How long do members stay in office?

ANSWER:
It depends on the district—usually two to three years. They can then decide to run again. Occasionally, in the middle of a term, people resign.

QUESTION:
I have been to board meetings where they say they are going into executive session. What is an executive session?

ANSWER:
When the members of the board want to discuss any personnel issues , they go into executive session. For example, the Board of Education may decide in "executive session" whether or not a teacher gets tenure. This would *not* be discussed where the general public could listen. The result of the executive session would be brought before the public. A general statement would be made. For example, "Tenure in the area of music is granted to Mrs. Jones beginning, today, March ____, 200_."

QUESTION:
There are things going on in my school that I think a board member should know about. Should I call a board member?

ANSWER:
As a beginning teacher, your perception is limited. Talk over the problem with a trusted colleague. Get some advice from someone who has been with the school system for a long period of time. As a beginning teacher, I would stay away from politics and concentrate on teaching.

QUESTION:
Can anyone go to a Board of Education meeting, or do you have to be a resident?

ANSWER:
Anyone can go to the meetings.

QUESTION:
Can I speak at the board meetings about an issue that is educationally related?

ANSWER:
Yes, you can. You usually have to "sign in " so the board president knows you wish to speak. S/he may then call your name and ask you to state your name and address. Some districts do not need you to register beforehand, but will ask if anyone has any board concerns. The time for the public to speak may happen at the beginning or end of the meeting. Remember, this must be a general educational issue.

QUESTION:
Do board members answer you immediately after you ask a question?

ANSWER:
Sometimes they answer, sometimes they don't. The person who will respond to your question is the board president. If your answer is not given right away, it may be discussed among the members in executive session and answered publicly by the board president after the board members have had an opportunity to meet and discuss the issue.

QUESTION:
Are teachers on the board?

ANSWER:
They can be on the board. Just like everyone else, they have to get voted in. If a teacher lives and works in the same district, it would be considered a conflict of interest to be on the BOE.

QUESTION:
I enjoy Christmas and all the festivities. Can I celebrate with the children?

ANSWER:
Know your board policy for holidays. Some schools will not allow you to celebrate the holidays because of the different religions of the children. Find out from your principal or fellow teachers what the policy is for holiday celebrations.

QUESTION:
I want to take my kids on a field trip, but it is very expensive. Can I have a fund raiser?

ANSWER:
You need to talk with your administrator. Your administrator will know what the board policy is on fund raisers. Also, some districts require that the field trip must have board approval before notes about the trip go home. A field trip may be refused by the Board of Education. Check your district policy before telling children about the trip.

Parents

Parents are a very important part of a child's education. They can make or break your job as a teacher. Some parents feel they pay taxes and all of the education of their child falls on the shoulders of the teachers. Some parents feel they pay taxes and know it is impossible for a teacher to meet the needs of all children. I have run into both types of parents. My philosophy is this: I do the best I can for all children. I contact all parents, even the ones I know I won't get a response from. It is my professional and moral obligation to treat all children and parents the same. I would encourage you to do the same.

QUESTION:

I have a parent who comes to my door every day and asks how her child is doing. It is becoming a problem. What do I do?

ANSWER:

You want to encourage parent participation, but you don't want to be strangled by it either. Talk to this parent. An example of the conversation could be:

> "Mrs. J. it seems like you are very concerned about your daughter's education. I wish all parents would be as concerned as you are. However, it is difficult to talk with you every morning because I am responsibile for all 26 of my children. Do you think you could write me a note, or stop by at the end of the week, if you have an urgent concern?"

At this point, you could have a variety of reactions. From a simple okay, to a more complex situation where you would have an angry parent. If the parent becomes angry, s/he may discuss the matter with your principal. Let's suppose your administrator does not agree with you and wants parents around all the time. In that case, you must find a way to tactfully avoid the situation. Keep yourself busy. Work with a student when you think this parent will be around. You can then say, "Mrs. J. I wish I could talk but I have a student who needs me now." Hopefully this parent will get the hint.

QUESTION:
I had a parent at my door during class time because she was mad at the way I disciplined her son. It disrupted my whole day. She wouldn't back off and I had other students in the room.

ANSWER:
Next time that happens, gently but firmly explain that you would be happy to speak with her, but you are responsible for the rest of the children in the class during the school day. She may become even more upset with you. But the bottom line is: *you* are responsible for 26 children one of which is her child. After she has left, quickly jot a note to your administrator to explain what happened. An administrator cannot support you if s/he doesn't know the facts. ALWAYS explain your side of the story.

QUESTION:
We have a parent organization in my school and many parents are actively involved. Should I attend the meetings too?

ANSWER:
This is entirely up to you. I have gone to some of the meetings because I was interested in what was on the agenda. You will usually find a very dedicated group of people who want to help their children in any way they can.

QUESTION:
Why does this parent group have fund raisers? What is the money used for?

ANSWER:
The parents recognize that many of the extras they want for their children cannot be purchased with school funds. Therefore, they hold fund raisers and use the profits to buy needed supplies and pay for educational programs for the school. Usually, it is a collective decision as to how to spend the money. This decision is made by the parents with suggestions from the principal and teachers.

QUESTION:
Do I have to buy candy from my students to help out the parent group?

ANSWER:
No, you'd go broke buying candy from all of your kids. I tell all of my students "no" when they ask me to buy candy. I do this so there are no hard feelings with any child.

QUESTION:
When should I let parents know their child is a candidate for retention?

ANSWER:
If a child is a candidate for retention, a parent should have been informed throughout the year about the child's progress. As the teacher, you should have kept careful records of each time you had spoken with this parent so there will be no surprises. Around the 30 week marking period, before talking to the parents, get clearance from your principal about retaining this child. A parent can refuse retention, but as the teacher you write in the permanent record card that the child was *placed* in the next year not *promoted*. You could also ask your administrator if the secretary can type up a letter like the following which will be signed by the parent.

> This letter is to inform the school that I do not want my child
>
> repeated this school year _____. I want my child to be in
>
> grade _____.
>
> Parent Signature_____ Date_____

QUESTION:
How often do I have to inform parents about their child's progress?

ANSWER:
Most schools have a 10 - 20 - 30 - 40 week progress report card. Some schools also have an additional 15 - 25 - 35 week report. If you feel a child is having a difficult time in school, you may need to contact that parent more often. Remember to *document* that you have contacted that parent. I have had many parents say, "I never knew that before. How come you didn't tell me?" Thanks to careful documentation, I was able to show them my index file where I had noted the exact day and time that I had informed this parent.

QUESTION:
Why do parents have the final say about retention?

ANSWER:
I haven't figured that out yet, but in some districts they do. You can suggest retention and usually parents will go along with you. However, there are situations where they do not. Make sure you document your recommendation in the permanent record card.

QUESTION:
I have a parent who I don't get along with and her child is in my room this year. How do I handle that?

ANSWER:
You separate your feelings about the parent from the child. It is very difficult to do, but it can be done. Remember this child is his own person. Don't prejudge the child because of the parent.

QUESTION:
Can parents bring in treats for their child's birthday?

ANSWER:
Some schools welcome treats and some schools don't . Some schools will let parents bake cookies. Other schools insist the treat must be bought and kept in its original package. Talk to your fellow colleagues to find out what the procedure is in your building.

Also, Make sure you know if any of your children have allergies to certain types of foods before the first birthday treat. Many children have allergies. It is up to you to know that information. You can usually find out from your school nurse. If a child has allergies to certain foods, ask the *parent* to give you "food substitutes" his/her child can eat during birthday time. In addition, some children get severe headaches because of perfume. As a teacher, be sensitive to this.

QUESTION:
So many of my parents want to know how to help their child at home and don't know what to do? How can I help them?

ANSWER:
It is wonderful having caring parents. What you can do is set one objective for the parents during a parent conference. For instance, let's look at math. Perhaps the child can count to 10, but gets confused when s/he attempts to count any higher. Your simple objective for the parents would be to help the child move from 10 through 15. (*Not* 10 through 100.) Keep the objective simple and provide strategies for the parents on how to help the child reach that goal.

QUESTION:
I had a parent invite me to her child's birthday party. I don't want to go, what do I do?

ANSWER:
Just explain that you make it a policy not to attend any parties for your children. When you are responsible for 26 children, it would be unrealistic to attend 26 parties. In my many years of teaching, I attended one child's First Communion party, and that was only because there were unusual circumstances with this child. Love your children, but keep your personal life separate from your professional life.

QUESTION:
I'm nervous about parent conferences. What do I say? How do I say it?

ANSWER:
I was intimidated by my first parent conference. Someone gave me good advice about conferences. He told me to use the sandwich method. No, I didn't know what he meant. The sandwich method is saying something nice about the child, saying whatever you feel needs to be corrected, then saying something nice about the child. I have followed this advice for years. The conversation may sound like this:

Teacher:	Mrs. Jones, thank you for coming in today. I really enjoy having your son in my room. He has a great sense of humor.
Mrs. Jones:	Thank you, not everyone appreciates him.
Teacher:	Sometimes, though, he says things that are hurtful to other children. I'm sure he doesn't mean it, but I have spoken to him and would like you to do so also.
Mrs. Jones:	What do you mean? What has he said?
Teacher:	He was telling a joke about kids who have smelly shoes and he said, "You know, like Mary's shoes."
Mrs. Jones:	I'm sorry, I apologize for his behavior. (That's the best case scenario. You could also hear, "Not my son.")
Teacher:	I appreciate his humor, but I don't want him to use it to hurt another child.
Mrs. Jones:	I'll speak with him.

Notice the sandwich effect. Say something good, say whatever the inappropriate behavior is, then say something good.

Another piece of advice is avoid buzz words. Parents don't know what you mean when you say SAT's, whole language, inclusion, math manipulatives, etc. Keep the language simple when talking to parents. You may also want to prepare youself for a conference by filling out a form like the one below for each child.

Student Name _____

Academic Strengths _____

_____

Academic Weaknesses _____

_____

Homework _____

Parental Concerns _____

_____

Decisions Reached _____

_____

Parental Signature _____

Date _____

QUESTION:
How do I cover all the needed academic concerns during a 15 minute conference?

ANSWER:
If a child is not having difficulty in math, you don't need to go over math. Use the sandwich method again. Tell the parent, "Mark is doing great in math and reading, but he doesn't turn his homework in. He also appears to need help when reading in the content area of social studies. I know he could do the work, he just needs to apply himself."

Make sure you have papers from the subject areas you are concerned with to show the parents. In addition, keep all those papers you have had parents sign stating they saw the paper. This helps at conference time if they were to tell you, "But you never told me."

QUESTION:
What about parents who everyone is afraid of because they become so irate if you even suggest their child is doing something wrong?

ANSWER:
You may want to have administrative support if you know a particular set of parents may give you a hard time. My first year of teaching was memorable for many reasons. One reason is I had a parent who had flaming red hair and her temper matched it.

Everyone but me knew about her until the first day of conferences. When she came to the building, everyone shut their own doors and my principal magically showed up in my room. Thank goodness she did, because I wouldn't have known how to handle her. If you are nervous about conferences, ask beforehand if there is a particular parent that may cause you some grief. If the answer is yes, find out how to handle this situation. You may only need another special area teacher in the room who can concur with what you are telling the parent. Another option is to invite the principal in for the conference. It is not a sign of weakness to have your administrator present. Just this past year, I had administrative support for a particular "sticky" conference.

QUESTION:
Is there any other way beside telephone that I can keep in contact with parents?

ANSWER:
Some teachers use a weekly newsletter. This newsletter contains all sorts of information, including field trip reminders, needed supplies for a project, book order reminders, a holiday festival schedule, etc.

Sample Newsletter

THE WEEK OF _____

In Reading we learned . . .	In Math we learned . . .
In Social Studies we learned . . .	In Science we learned . . .

Please remember to . . .

Our daily schedule is:

Monday	Library
Tuesday	Gym
Wednesday	Art
Thursday	Music
Friday	Gym

School Related Personnel (SRP)

In the district I work in, School Related Personnel are people that help your building run smoothly, but aren't teachers. For example, secretaries, teacher aides, janitors, bus drivers, monitors, and cafeteria workers are all considered SRP.

QUESTION:
Are the secretaries, teacher aides, janitors. etc. always called school related personnel?

ANSWER:
No, another name may be given. This group of people has a different union representing them. They work under a different pay schedule and different hours than that of teachers.

QUESTION:
My room needs a new light. Do I tell the janitor?

ANSWER:
In some buildings you can just ask the janitor to change the light. In other buildings, you need to put in a work order and submit it to the principal. The procedure varies, so check it out with a colleague. Unfortunately, sometimes it takes longer to go through the procedures than it does to change the light bulb.

QUESTION:
I am working on a paper for college. Can I have the secretary type it?

ANSWER:
Secretaries are *not* required to do paper work that is not school related. That would be your responsibility. You may ask a secretary to type a letter that is school related business. For example, a field trip permission slip is school related.

QUESTION:
One of my students is a child of a School Related Personnel. I'm uncomfortable with this because I also see this family out of school. What do I do?

ANSWER:
If you find this out before school starts, you may want to explain to your principal how you feel. Some principals will move the child out of your room. If this doesn't happen, explain to the parents that you are in an awkward position, but their child will be treated just like everyone else's child. If these people are friends, you'll remain friends.

QUESTION:

The bus driver yelled at me in front of the kids. He told me he wouldn't put a child on the bus because that child had been removed for inappropriate behavior. What do I do?

ANSWER:

First of all, you should know when a child is removed from a bus. But since you didn't know, you did nothing wrong. Go to the bus driver privately and tell this person not to talk to you unprofessionally. If this person is still disagreeable you may want to talk to your principal. Bus drivers have a very, very tough job. Imagine trying to teach with your back to all of the kids. A bus driver performs with all children behind him, not in front where the driver could see. You may have caught this driver at a bad moment. The behavior was wrong, but sometimes people do things they regret afterwards. Give this person the benefit of the doubt.

QUESTION:

I have been assigned a teacher's aide for two hours per day. How do I best utilize this person?

ANSWER:

It all depends on how you run your class. If your children are up and about during the day, you may want to have your aide monitor them while you do some individualized teaching. Or you may want to have your aide work with a child who seems to be having a difficult time understanding a concept. It is up to you how to maximize this person's talents.

QUESTION:

The teacher aide I have doesn't know how to teach and she is driving me crazy. What do I do?

ANSWER:

People have different talents. Figure out the talents of this person. Perhaps she could put up bulletin boards for you, run off copies of papers you'll need, or correct papers. Think about all you do and find a purposeful option for your aide.

QUESTION:

My aide wants to run my room. How do I set limits?

ANSWER:

You have answered your own question. *You* set the limits. Explain that you are ultimately responsible for the children and therefore, you will make the rules. Believe me, it is easier said than done. But it must be done.

QUESTION:

I have a wonderful teacher's aide. I don't want to lose her, but the administrators decide every year who works together. Is there anything I can do to have this person back?

ANSWER:

You can try talking to your administrator and explain that you have a wonderful working relationship with this person which is benefiting the kids. That's about the best you can do. Some administrators listen, some don't.

QUESTION:

I don't know who has allergies to certain foods. Where do I get this information?

ANSWER:

The best place to start is your school nurse. The nurse will have a file on each child and that file will hold needed information about allergies. In the beginning of the year, the nurse at my school notifies us if any child has allergies so we know to avoid certain treats for that child. Sometimes the kids themselves will tell you, "I can't eat peanut butter, I get hives and can't breathe." Also, be careful with the type of perfume you wear. Some children get headaches from perfume and cologne.

QUESTION:
Can the nurse give kids medicine?

ANSWER:
Yes, if the child has a signed note from the doctor stating the need for that medication. You *cannot* give the medicine. If there was ever a reaction to a drug, the nurse would know what to do in an emergency.

QUESTION:
I have a child with many medical needs. I don't feel equipped to handle them. Help!!

ANSWER:
The downside of inclusion is that if a medically fragile child is placed in your regular classroom, you need to learn what to do should an emergency occur. Find out what to do during those precious minutes when the nurse is on the way to your room. The nurse is the person who will take care of the needs of the child. However, you will need to know how to contact the nurse for *immediate* help. The most important thing to do during an emergency is to keep your cool. I know this is hard to do. As for myself, I can react during an emergency, but I fall totally apart once the crisis is over.

QUESTION:
Can I get medicine for myself from the nurse?

ANSWER:
The nurse doesn't have medicine for individuals. If you have a headache and need an aspirin, you are better off asking a colleague. You are putting the nurse in an awkward position because she has to say no.

QUESTION:
What about girls who get their period? Can they get a pad from the nurse?

ANSWER:
Yes, just send them down with a note to avoid any embarrassment for the child. The nurse usually has pads in her office.

QUESTION:
How do I remember everyone's name? My building has over 60 adults working in it.

ANSWER:
It's impossible to remember everyone. I suggest you write down the names of the secretaries and janitors because they are the people who you will see and need every day. They are the people who know what is allowed and what isn't allowed.

Teacher's Union

The Teachers' Union is an organization that looks out for your interests. In most schools, unions are closed shop which means all must belong. In some districts, you have a choice. Given the choice, I would definately *become a member of the union.*

QUESTION:
Why should I become a member of the teachers' union?

ANSWER:
I know I asked myself that question when I first began teaching. To me it seemed like an awful lot of money, and I didn't know what I was getting back in return. After teaching for many years, I understand the importance of the union. Let's suppose that you have a principal who doesn't like you. It has nothing to do with your teaching, but there is a definite personality clash. Your principal could try and get rid of you. With union protection, it becomes difficult for your principal to dismiss you without just cause.

QUESTION:
How do I find out what my rights are?

ANSWER:
You need to get a copy of your contract. Usually you get a contract from a union representative. If you don't have a contract, ask for one. Included in this contract will be length of school day, number of sick days per year, number of personal days per year, length of school year, tuition reimbursement, salary schedule, etc. There is a lot of information in your contract. Take some time, read it over, and ask questions about items you don't understand.

QUESTION:
If there is an injustice done, how does the union protect me?

ANSWER:
There is a procedure that needs to be followed if there is a problem. Every building has a union representative. This person will help explain the procedure for filing a complaint. However, as a first year teacher, talk to a union representative about the situation. Usually, problems can be solved without a grievance. Veteran teachers will have suggestions for you. Ask them.

QUESTION:
What is a grievance?

ANSWER:
A grievance is a written statement explaining to your boss how the contract is being broken.

QUESTION:
If I put in a grievance, does that anger the boss and potentially make my life more miserable?

ANSWER:
Yes, as a first year teacher, stay miserable over the problem you are facing. Don't file a grievance. If you had tenure, then you could try and seek out a mutual solution.

QUESTION:
What happens if my boss denies any wrong doing?

ANSWER:
Your union representatives will decide if they want to take it to the next step. The next step involves bringing the matter before the Board of Education.

QUESTION:
Do I have to pay for this grievance procedure?

ANSWER:
No, that's what you pay union dues for.

QUESTION:
What happens if the board sides with the administrator and not with me?

ANSWER:
That happens all the time. The union can then determine whether or not they should go to arbitration . This process involves people who are not associated with the district. This is costly, so unions only go to arbitration if they feel they will win your case.

QUESTION:
Do unions get along with administration?

ANSWER:
Some do, some don't. It all depends upon the personalities of the people involved.

QUESTION:
Have you always belonged to the union?

ANSWER:
When I worked in a private school, I didn't have a union. Presently I'm working in a public school, and yes, I belong to the union.

QUESTION:
What do unions do besides fight for your rights?

ANSWER:
That keeps them pretty busy. But they also send money to Albany (New York State union) to lobby for teachers' rights for New York State. Your state may send money to your lobbying organization.

QUESTION:
What is tenure and why is the union fighting to keep tenure?

ANSWER:

Tenure is earned by a teacher for competency in teaching. In some states it takes three years to earn tenure. The amount of time required to receive tenure varies state to state. Once you have tenure, you cannot be dismissed from your job unless you are incompetent. Let's suppose you have been teaching for three years and the principal decides s/he wants a different person in your position. If you have tenure and have been proven to be competent, a principal *cannot* ask you to leave. It's that simple.

QUESTION:

What is the procedure for obtaining tenure?

ANSWER:

This would vary, but I'll speak from my experience. As a beginning teacher, I was observed by my administrator several times for three years. In addition, I was observed by the assistant superintendent and director of education. After watching me teach, they would sit and discuss what they had observed. This observation was put in writing. When I had completed three years of teaching, I was recommended for tenure since all parties involved were pleased with my teaching. A recommendation that I receive tenure was brought before the Board of Education. It is very stressful to have people watch you teach, but everyone goes through it.

QUESTION:

What is renewable tenure?

ANSWER:

The unions have been fighting against renewable tenure. Renewable tenure is when a district can *renew* your *tenure* every five years. So, after five years, if they decide they don't want you, they can get rid of you. Maybe they like you for the first five years, but decide you are getting too expensive after ten years. They could decide not to *renew* your *tenure*. So, you can see why tenure is a debated educational issue.

QUESTION:

I have heard parents say "Teachers have it made once they get their tenure." Is that true?

ANSWER:

This is not at all true. Teachers have to show competency every year. They are evaluated every year by the principal. It is costly to remove a teacher, but it can be done. You must stay competent. It makes sense to do your job the best you can.

QUESTION:

I have an option to join or not join the union. What would you do?

ANSWER:

Join, you'll never regret it. You will receive the same benefits as paying members. However, your colleagues may become angry because they are paying your way when you don't join.

QUESTION:

I have just been hired at a public school and the contract between the Board of Education and teachers has not been renewed. What does that mean for me?

ANSWER:

It means the old contract language is still in effect. Unfortunately, it also means that tension exists between the Board of Education and teachers. Teachers are not allowed to strike without severe penalty. But there are certain things tenured teachers will do to draw attention to their unhappiness. Be careful. If you are untenured, don't do anything to jeopardize your job. I have observed non-tenured teachers walking a picket line. This is not a good idea.

QUESTION:
Why isn't it a good idea to walk a picket line? I want to support the teachers.

ANSWER:
The principal makes a recommendation for your tenure after the allotted time of teaching. The Board of Education accepts this recommendation. You don't want to draw negative attention to yourself. Legally, you are allowed to walk the picket line. But practically, it's just not a wise choice. You may be unjustly labeled as a troublemaker. Keep a low profile. When I began teaching, I walked into a situation where the teachers did not have a contract. Fortunately, someone pulled me aside and explained the rules of the game. I will forever be indebted to this person.

QUESTION:
How is a contract ratified? What is the procedure?

ANSWER:
Teachers and board members are the individuals that comprise the "negotiating team". They try to come up with a mutually agreed upon contract. Board members are looking for the needs of the taxpayers, and teachers are looking out for teacher needs. Unfortunately, the needs vary and agreement can sometimes take two to three years. Once both parties have agreed upon the contract, the teacher members of the negotiating team will present the contract to the rest of the teachers in the union. If the teachers vote to pass the contract, the Board of Education has to vote to pass the contract too. Since board members are on the negotiating team, it's usually a necessary formality for the board to pass the contract. You will see many smiling faces once a contract has been ratified. Tenured and non-tenured teachers are all happy it's over.

QUESTION:
How many years is a contract?

ANSWER:
That varies, I have had three year contracts and the longest I've had is five years.

QUESTION:
What if I don't like a teacher on the team I'm working with? I don't agree with her philosophy of education, especially the way she treats the children . Should I talk to my union?

ANSWER:
My advice, and it may be hard to swallow, is keep your mouth closed. Don't stir up trouble between colleagues. It is the administrator's responsibility to discuss teaching styles with the teacher, not yours. There will be teachers who you don't agree with. Be pleasant, build bridges, don't build walls. If there comes a time when it is suggested that you share an activity with this teacher's class, make yourself unavailable. Teacher bashing is not something a union gets involved with. The union looks out for the good of all teachers. They do not single anyone out.

Substitute Teacher

It is important to know what to do should you need to call for a substitute. This chapter will help you prepare for that day.

QUESTION:
Who do I call if I'm sick and can't come to school?

ANSWER:
This is something you need to find out BEFORE you are sick. The calling in procedure varies from district to district. In one district I had to call the school secretary to let her know I wouldn't be in on a particular day. If I knew very early in the morning, or the evening before, I would leave a message on an answering machine. In another district, I had to call an 800 number and use the prompts to answer the questions about my illness.

QUESTION:
Can I select the substitute I want for my classsroom?

ANSWER:
This will vary from district to district. In one district, I have to have phone numbers of the substitute I'm requesting. At the prompt, I have to punch in the phone number of the substitute. In some districts, you can request a particular substitute, but someone else may make the decision as to who will be in for you. In some schools, substitutes need to be pre-approved by the Board of Education before they can begin teaching. This is another area you want to know about BEFORE you need it.

QUESTION:
What do I need to leave for a substitute?

ANSWER:
You need to leave plans for the substitute to follow. Most districts require teachers to keep planbooks. A substitute will follow these plans. In one building I've worked at, all teachers must keep a "Substitute Folder".

QUESTION:
What do you keep in your substitute folder?

ANSWER:
This folder contains:
1. Daily schedule
2. Rough time frame of daily happenings. For example . . .
    9:00-9:15   Attendance
    9:15-9:30   Morning Announcements

> 9:30-10:30   Reading/Writing
> 10:30-11:30   Math

3. Children's names who may be on regular medication
4. Children's names who may have medical condition i.e. mild seizures, allergic reactions
5. Any bus/hall responsibilities that you have
6. Generic Plans

QUESTION:
What are generic plans?

ANSWER:
Generic plans are plans that can be followed easily and at any time of the year. They are not specific, but yet purposeful. For example, I have left a book for a substitute to read. As a follow up activity, I have asked her to have the children write about their favorite part and draw a picture. I have also had them write out five questions about the story. Everyone does this assignment, no matter what reading group he or she is in. It's "generic", all kids can complete the assignment.

For math, you could leave sheets that are below grade level. This could serve as a review for the students. The substitute wouldn't have to worry about teaching a new concept.

The more you are prepared for your sub, the better it is for everyone, including you. When you get back, you don't want piles of papers everywhere.

QUESTION:
Do children behave for a substitute?

ANSWER:
Unfortunately, they usually don't. For this very reason, before I need a substitute, I talk to my children about respect for the substitute teacher. I tell my kids if I get any notes about bad behavior, I will follow up on them. Despite telling them this, I still get notes. I always follow up and talk to the children who have been disrespectful.

QUESTION:
What if there is a substitute in my room and I don't like what was done? Can I do anything about it?

ANSWER:
This varies from school to school. You may want to talk with a colleague. You may be able to request NOT to have certain people in your room. Sometimes requests are honored, sometimes they aren't.

QUESTION:
How do I let the substitute know the rules of the classroom?

ANSWER:
You could set this up ahead of time. You will come to know your student's strengths and weaknesses. You will find a responsible child who can explain the routines in your room. This child can have the title of "substitute helper." All children will know who this person is. When there is a sub. in the room, "Mary, the substitute helper" will explain the rules of the room.

QUESTION:
Why do I need a substitute aid?

ANSWER:
When you aren't there, kids are not themselves. They will try to get away with things.

If you have the "substitute aid", this student can make the teaching day run smoother.

The more you are prepared for your sub, the better it is for everyone, including you. When you get back, follow through on any "substitute" notes.

QUESTION:
Are there any other survival tips?

ANSWER:
Yes, I'll list them for you.

1. Leave your room ready for a substitute daily. No one plans on getting a fever at 2 in the morning. It just happens. So, be prepared. Every day when you leave your room, leave it as if you won't be back the next day.

2. Check off items in your planbook that you have completed. It makes it easier for the sub to figure out what needs to be done.

3. If you want a paper kept in school, make sure the substitute knows that. You might have a valuable test going home, never to be seen again.

4. Before you leave school, put your morning message on the board. That's one less thing a substitute will have to worry about.

QUESTION:
What do I need to do when I return to school?

ANSWER:
Read all the notes the substitute left you. If a child was particularly troublesome, do something about it. Children will be watching what you do. Let all kids know you won't accept unacceptable behavior.

QUESTION:
How will I know if my objectives have been met for the day?

ANSWER:
Included in your substitute folder, you could have a form that you ask the substitute to fill out. Some subs come prepared with their own form. The form may look like this:

Substitute Name_____

Today's Date_____

If possible, please follow the plans in my planbook. If not, feel free to use the "Generic plans" in this folder. Please use a check mark to indicate that you have completed an assignment.

Please do not have the children take any of their papers home. I want to look at them.

Your helper of the day will be "Mary". She is a very responsible child. She knows all the routines.

If any child is particularly disobedient, please let me know. I want to talk with the child who breaks the classroom rules.

Enjoy the kids. They are a great bunch.

Joanna

Getting to Know

Your Students

Younger Children

When you teach children, you automatically give yourself permission to be a child. You'll laugh when they laugh, and you'll want to cry when they cry.

QUESTION:
How do I get to know my students?

ANSWER:
There are many ways to get to know your students. Here is one example. Get a sheet of paper and fold it in half, and then in half again. At the top left write "My Name is_____. " In the top right box, write "My Favorite Food is." In the bottom left box, write "With my family, I like to . . .". In the bottom right box, write "My Favorite Pet is . . ." This can obviously vary, but it gives you a good start. Then walk around the room and talk to your children about what they drew. They could also write a little about their picture.

Sample Get-Acquainted Paper	
My Name is . . .	My favorite food is . . .
With my family, I like to . . .	My pet is . . .

If a child doesn't have a pet, have this child draw a pet they would like to have. That opens up a lot of discussion.

QUESTION:
How do I teach my children responsibility?

ANSWER:
This is a tough thing to do unless you have parent support. I know many times I have given children a paper to complete at home and it comes back not completed, or doesn't come back at all. I give my students the benefit of the doubt the first time they forget. After that, there are consequences for irresponsibility. For example, perhaps I had been planning on playing a game with the class. A child who consistently forgets will not play the game. If the child still doesn't return an assignment, I will telephone home and

talk to the parents about the child's lack of responsibility. Some parents appreciate the phone call, some don't. Another procedure I have seen work efficiently is when two or three teachers team together and have a certain time of day when they have a "work" room and a "game" room. If a child does not finish his work, he is assigned to the "work" room. A child who completes everything is assigned to the "game" room. What the children don't seem to realize is that the games are all educational. They're still learning, therefore it's not a waste of time.

QUESTION:
What do I do when students tell me things about their family that I know they shouldn't be telling me?

ANSWER:
When a child begins to tell family secrets, I look at them and ask, "Would your mom want you to be telling me this?" If the child says no, I gently explain how some things stay in the family. I've also heard a child say, "I don't know if my mom would care." If that is the case, I tell them since they aren't sure, maybe they had better not tell me. But as a teacher, you need to *listen* for warning signs of possible abuse in the family. If there is abuse, you need to contact the Child Abuse Hot line. It is your professional obligation to contact this hot line.

QUESTION:
I feel the children will think I'm unapproachable if I don't listen. What do you think?

ANSWER:
I always listen to my kids. However, I don't ask questions and I'm careful if I feel they are telling me things that are family business.

QUESTION:
One of my students died unexpectedly. How do I handle this with the children?

ANSWER:
Don't be afraid to show that you are upset! Explain to the children this is a hard time for everyone. Invite them to talk about how they feel. Reassure them that death usually doesn't happen so quickly. They will be afraid of their own mortality.

QUESTION:
I have a child who is terminally ill. All of the children know. Have you ever had to handle that situation?

ANSWER:
Unfortunately, yes I have had to handle this. Since I work in a public school, I'm not permitted to discuss my religious beliefs. So when the topic of illness is brought up, I listen and offer hope. My students have learned to appreciate the little things in life. We have also made things for the sick child. This comforts my children and hopefully lightens the burden of the child who is suffering.

QUESTION:
One of my students is very self-directed, but when her mother is in the room, she acts helpless. Any suggestions?

ANSWER:
Talk to your student privately and tell her what you expect of her at all times. Talk about consequences for acting helpless. I would also speak with the mom and explain how her daughter is just acting helpless, and that she is a very capable little girl.

QUESTION:
I have a child whose parents are going through a divorce. This happy child appears to be very sullen lately. What can I do?

ANSWER:
I would call the parents and explain what you are seeing in school. Keep the conversation as objective as you can. Do *not* take the side of either parent. Explain how you are only interested in their child. Offer school counseling if you have a school counselor. Usually you have to have parental permission before a child can talk with the counselor.

QUESTION:
I have a student I really enjoy. I try not to show favoritism, but it's hard. Any suggestions?

ANSWER:
There are just some kids that seem to draw the best out of us, aren't there? Their smile brings on your smile. I try to treat all students the same, but I'm not sure I'm always successful. All I can tell you is since you are aware of what you are doing, try to be fair to *all* students. This particular student may have a special place in your heart, but other students will quickly dislike him/her if you show favoritism.

QUESTION:
I have a student no one likes. What can I do?

ANSWER:
This happens every year. There is always a student kids alienate for one reason or another. I have talked with my students about the child when the child is not around. We discuss feelings and how it is so important to treat people kindly. After the discussion, you will usually see a few kids trying very hard to make the unwanted child wanted.

QUESTION:
What if the unwanted child is mean to the other kids?

ANSWER:
This happens too, and it's sad. What I have done is talk with the outsider alone and try to get to the bottom of the behavior. I have also called in our school counselor and parents of the child when I feel I'm at a loss as to what to do. There are some children that, no matter how hard you try, they prefer to treat people unfavorably.

QUESTION:
What do I do if a child is sick and needs to go to the nurse? I can't leave the rest of the children unattended in the room.

ANSWER:
If a child is ill, you can usually get another child to walk the sick person to the nurse's office. If you feel the child is too ill to go alone or with a friend, use your intercom and ask the office for assistance. Explain that you have a sick child who cannot make it to the nurse on his/her own. Be specific as to what the problem is. The nurse may have to bring the emergency medical bag or wheelchair to your room.

QUESTION:
What if a child has a nosebleed? What do I do?

ANSWER:
You do *not* touch the child's blood unless you have protective gloves on. Hand the child a tissue and model for the child where he needs to squeeze his nose. Once you

have your gloves on, you can help the child pinch the nose. *Never* touch a child's blood. There are too many diseases transferred through contact with blood.

QUESTION:
A child told me something his parent needs to know. What do I do?

ANSWER:
Explain to the child that you are responsible for him/her. With this responsibility there are things that a parent must know. Communicate to the child that you are doing what is best for him/her. Tell the child you are informing the parents because you care. You will usually hear, "But I'll get in trouble." My response to this is, "You'll get in worse trouble if I don't tell them." Use your judgment as to what a parent needs to know. Some things you can solve with the child without a parent knowing.

QUESTION:
Can you give me some examples of what a parent needs to know?

ANSWER:
You might have a child tell you they took some cigarettes out of their mom's purse for a friend. You need to explain that what s/he did was wrong and the mom needs to know. If the child is upset, tell the child you will tell the mother that the child *is* sorry and upset. Most parents will appreciate that the child has told the truth about an unpleasant situation. Another example would be when a child tells you he 'accidentally' took $20 from his dad's wallet and his dad thought he took $10 for the school carnival. Now this child may have intentionally taken the $20, but help the child out of this situation. Using the same scenario, tell the parent how upset their child is and how the child realizes s/he made a mistake. Remember children are testing not only you, but parents as well. Help them to grow to be responsible adults, especially when they have made a mistake and are willing to admit it.

QUESTION:
Kids have told me, "Now, I'm going to be punished if you call home and tell my mom." What do I say to that comment?

ANSWER:
Explain that when people do wrong things, there is usually a punishment that goes along with it. Help the child to understand that the punishment will help him/her re-member not to do the wrong thing again.

QUESTION:
What are examples of times I don't need to tell a parent?

ANSWER:
Children will tell you a lot. They usually tell you more than what you want to know. My rule of thumb as to whether or not it is necessary to involve a parent is imagine *you* are a parent, would you want to know this about your child? If the answer is yes, call the parent.

QUESTION:
What do you think is *the* most important factor when teaching children?

ANSWER:
The most important thing to me is to treat children with *respect* at all times. They know when you mean it and they will act accordingly.

Older Children: Grades 4-5
Transitioning to Grade 6

Although most of the practices listed below can be duplicated no matter what grade a child is in, this chapter is directed to older children in grades four and five. At this age, children are becoming less dependent on the teacher and more inter-dependent on their peers.

QUESTION:

I have students that are not behaving and I don't know what to do? I have tried behavioral modifications, but they seem to work for only a short time. Any suggestions?

ANSWER:

Sometimes kids need to stay after school or come in early for "detention". Kids dislike staying late, or coming in early. Find out what your policy is in your particular building. Let the children know that you will enforce this policy and then make sure you *do*. If you don't enforce the policy, kids will take advantage of you.

QUESTION:

I sent home an unfavorable note to a parent and never received the signed copy I requested. What do I do?

ANSWER:

First of all, are you sure the parent received the note? Some kids will "forget" or "lose" the note. Before you call home, ask the child for specifics as to what happened to the note. Then, inform the child you will be calling home to check up on that version of the story. Usually this is when the truth comes out. If the child admits to not showing the note to his parent, you can do one of two things. You can give this child another chance by giving another note, or you can call home and tell the parent what happened. It's up to you. I like to give children the benefit of the doubt the first time around. I'm not as nice for the second offense. Also, make sure you make a copy of all notices that go home. File them in the child's individual folder. If the need arises, the note will be easy to photocopy should it become "lost" again.

What if the note did get home and the parents are angry with you about the note? You need to speak with your administrator and come up with a mutually agreed upon solution for the problem. You can't let this slide.

QUESTION:

I have some wonderful children. I'd love to take them bowling some evening. These kids don't get out much. Is that appropriate?

ANSWER:
Your intentions are wonderful. You are taking your job above and beyond the call of duty. However, I need to caution you. While you are with children in school, you are protected by the school insurance policy and your union. If a child gets hurt off school grounds, it will be your responsibility to take care of this child. Also, what if the child claims sexual harassment? I know this may seem far fetched, but it *could* happen. Although you are innocent, your name will be all over the newspaper. I have children I would love to take places. I have always made a decision on the side of caution. My advice is enjoy your children in school, but don't take them anywhere after hours unless their parent is going to supervise and drive them to the destination. Then "maybe" I would do it.

QUESTION:
My fifth graders have to move from class to class and are complaining because they can't use their backpacks? Why can't they use backpacks?

ANSWER:
Some schools have made a rule of not allowing children to carry backpacks. One of the reasons given was that backpacks are heavy and children could injure their backs. Another reason is backpacks could carry a weapon or drugs.

QUESTION:
I have lunch duty and I see some children sitting alone. It breaks my heart when other children don't include them. Is there anything I can do?

ANSWER:
With older children, it may be safer *not* to do anything. By your drawing attention to this loner and asking other children to include him/her they may pick on this loner even more, especially when you aren't around. You could offer a friendly smile, chat a few minutes and try to find out what this child's interests are. Perhaps if you notice a few children sitting alone, offer to have them sit together once you have talked to them individually to find out what their interests are. You could be the person who gets them on friendly terms. For instance, you could say, "Mary likes soccer and so do you Pete," or "You are both in fifth grade, do you want to sit together?" They may say no, or they may say yes. You never know until you've tried.

QUESTION:
My student wants to know if he can bring his cousin to school. Is this allowed?

ANSWER:
Check out your school policy before telling a kid yes. Usually it's not a problem, but check it out first.

QUESTION:
My student wants to bring his dog to school since we are studying about animals. His dog has gone to dog obedience school and we have been discussing dog obedience. Is this okay?

ANSWER:
Children have allergies and a child may have an allergy to dog hair. You also need to check out your school policy regarding animals. I know my kids have asked to bring in their dogs. I tell them to bring in a picture since our school policy is no dogs.

QUESTION:
Some of my kids have lice. Can I get lice?

ANSWER:
You sure can. When the nurse comes around to check heads, be the first head in line. I have a rule in my room: no child can sit in my seat. I have my chair labeled with my name. They know they must not sit there. Lice usually are found in the hair. So, if they rub their head against my chair, I could get lice. How can you control lice? Tell the children not to share combs and not to put on each other's hats or jackets. If lice are found in your room, use a strong disinfectant to clean off the chairs and desks. If a child is sent home due to lice, make sure this child goes to the nurse *before* returning to your class. A parent may have missed something that the nurse catches on the child's hair.

QUESTION:
I have good students who deserve recognition. Any suggestions?

ANSWER:
It's important to maintain parental contact. Telephone home and leave a message if no one is there. A quick, "Mrs. Jones, I really enjoy your son/daughter. S/he's such a good worker. I'm glad I've had the opportunity to teach her/him. " I set a goal to call one parent per week with a happy message. However, I don't always reach my goal. But it is always part of my "to do" list.

QUESTION:
I suspect a child is being physically abused. What do I do?

ANSWER:
Be very attentive to what children say to you. I had a child tell me his dad burnt him with a cigarette. Before jumping to any conclusions, I asked him how it happened. The student said, "Oh I was leaning back on my chair with my hands spread out like this and my dad *accidentally* (his word/not mine) burnt me." This is an example of how my conclusions were different from what happened.

When my son was five years old, he fell off his bike and landed on the concrete face down. His face was badly bruised. His eye was black and blue and there were plenty of scratches on his face. After my son got on the morning bus, I called school and explained to his teacher what happened.

I bring up these two incidence to show that *not* all situations are child abuse. But, if you suspect a child is being abused, you are required to report the situation. I know teachers in NY State are Mandated Reporters. and N.Y. State has an 800 number. Check your local phone book for the child abuse hot line in your area.

Before you pick up the phone, you may want to discuss the matter with a third party to get an objective view of a situation. You may be very emotionally involved with the student. Your principal or school counselor may have some information about this family that you have not been privy to up to this point. Maybe child protective services is already on this case. Perhaps the mother or father of this child is in the process of leaving home to live in a shelter for battered women/men. There are many different scenarios. I'm not trying to tell you *not* to call. I am trying to convey that things may be happening that you are unaware of.

QUESTION:
I have a student who comes from a good family. However, I've noticed he's beginning to hang around with kids who are in trouble a lot. Should I do anything?

ANSWER:
This is a very sensitive issue. Although we all have opinions of people, you cannot discuss the integrity of a student with parents of another student. But what can you do? Perhaps this child who comes from a "good" home is not doing the school work and the

grades are falling. Perhaps you've noticed this child is becoming a bit disrespectful. That *is* something you could mention to the parents. The parents may be unaware of the fact that their child is keeping company with tough kids. The parent may ask if there is something going on in school that they don't know about. At that point, you could mention that you've noticed their child is with a different group of children. You cannot judge these children , but you can state the facts. Every year I ask my son's teachers what kind of kids my son spends time with. Since I ask, they can tell me. But not all parents know to ask. So, you need to help them along.

QUESTION:
I have a student who told me he did his homework, but I don't think he's telling me the truth. How can I get him to confess?

ANSWER:
I run into this quite a bit. Usually the conversation goes like this:

Teacher   Joe, where is your homework.

Joe   I did it, but I left it at home.

Teacher   Where exactly did you leave it?

Joe   I think I left it in my bedroom.

Teacher   Okay, so if I call home, I can ask your mom to look in the bedroom?

Joe   She's not home, she's at work.

Teacher   Oh, that's okay, I'll call later.

Joe   She won't be home until real, real late.

Teacher   Joe, do you want to tell me something different about your homework?

Joe   No

Teacher   Okay

(Joe is looking very uneasy. He is fidgeting.)

Teacher   Hey Joe, we all make mistakes. It is easier to tell the truth. Do you want to tell me something different about your homework?

Joe   Yeah, I didn't do it. Don't call my mom.

Teacher   You know what Joe, I won't. Hand it in tomorrow. But next time, tell me the truth the first time around, or I will call your mom.

Joe   Yeah.

The next time will come around. Joe may or may not tell you the truth. But if he doesn't tell you the truth, follow through with the phone call. It all comes back to "say what you mean and mean what you say" when teaching children. Also, the other kids in the class are watching how you are handling the situation. If you treat the situation as a mistake, kids usually rise to the occasion. I have overheard kids telling other kids, "Don't lie to Mrs. Torreano, she always finds out. Just tell her the truth, she's nicer that way." Another scenario is a child who is consistently telling stories. The children watch how I handle it. Although I don't like his exaggerations, I have to keep in mind where this child is coming from and help him to grow to be a better person. That's what your job is too, helping children learn from all their mistakes.

QUESTION:

I have a student who regularly sees the school counselor. He is in fifth grade. In the beginning of the school year, he was eager to leave the room and talk. We are seven months into the schoolyear and this child *appears* to be embarrassed when the counselor comes to the door. Any suggestions?

ANSWER:

Children change and become more aware of what their peers are saying about them. Perhaps you could suggest to the counselor that you set up a specific time to meet with this student. When the time comes, quietly go over to this student and tell him it's time to talk to the counselor. If you are like me, you'll forget to remind the student. A helpful hint is to purchase a timer. Set the timer for when the child has to leave. When the timer rings, the child is on his way. You can also set the timer for students who have to leave for speech, reading, occupational therapy etc.

QUESTION:

I have a student who consistently asks me for directions on how to do an assignment once I've gone over the directions for everyone in the class. He's capable of doing the assignment on his own. He's seeking attention. It is becoming very irritating.

ANSWER:

I know that feeling. To eliminate your frustration, have another student explain what needs to be done. If this child is seeking attention from you, perhaps you could spend some time in the morning just chatting with this student.

QUESTION:

I have a student who takes things from other kids' desks. This child has been caught and confronted, but still continues to take things. Any suggestions?

ANSWER:

Take this child aside and see if you can figure out *why* s/he is acting inappropriately. Is the child taking money? Maybe s/he feels s/he needs to buy something and the parents are not giving any money to her/him. This does *not* make it right, but it does provide an explanation as to why the child is taking money from other kids. Once you understand the problem, you can work at a solution. Is the child taking pencils, pens and erasers? Again, find out why. Try talking to this child alone to determine why s/he is taking things that don't belong to her/him.

If the child continues to take things from other children, it's time to inform the parents. This could go either way. You could hear, "Not my child, how dare you." Or, "Thank you for telling us." If you get the first response, be prepared to explain everything to your administrator. In fact, you should probably make your administrator aware of the situation BEFORE you call the parents. I know I've said it before but it is worth repeating.. An administrator can't help or support you if they don't know there is a problem.

QUESTION:

I have a child who is eager to answer questions in class, but the answers are always inappropriate. For example, I asked what a compound word was and this child answered, "I went skating with my mom and dad yesterday." This happens a lot. I don't even want to call on this child. Any ideas?

ANSWER:

This is a child who is seeking attention and will do whatever needs to be done to win some. You could try talking to this child privately and explain what you are hearing.

(Wrong answers!) You could ask this child to raise his hand only when he thinks he has an answer to your question. Since this child is obviously seeking your notice, maybe you would want to have some "talk time" in the beginning of the day with this child. But tell this child that "talk time" with be discontinued if he continues to give inappropriate answers to your questions. If he looks like he doesn't know what you are talking about, model for him what he says. He'll probably smirk. Kids usually get it when they hear themselves speak.

QUESTION:
My kids are always blaming someone else when things go wrong in the room. There is so much finger pointing, I'm not sure who did what. Help!

ANSWER:
When this happens, it's time to sit everyone down and talk about respect and kindness. Talk about how you want them to treat each other. Talk about the rules of the room. Explain that sometimes we make mistakes and break a rule. Teach them it's okay to occasionally break a rule, but it's not okay to blame someone else for something you've done. Then ask if there is anyone who needs to apologize for something. Usually you'll get kids with hands in the air and admitting to whatever the wrongdoing was. However, sometimes it doesn't work. There are just some kids who are very difficult to get through to. However, you will get through to the majority of your kids.

Ways of Learning

It is important to determine how a student learns so that teaching is more child centered. When I began teaching, I didn't know anything about learning methods. Reading books and talking with colleagues has helped me to grow in this area. If you are interested in reading books on learning styles, check out the suggested readings at the end of this book.

QUESTION:
What do you mean by ways in which you learn?

ANSWER:
People gather and interpret information in different ways. The way you gather and interpret information is the way you learn.

QUESTION:
What are the different ways in which to learn?

ANSWER:
The four *major* learning methods are:
1. Visual Learner
2. Auditory Learner
3. Tactile Learner
4. Kinesthetic Learner

QUESTION:
What are the differences between them?

ANSWER:
A visual learner is someone who learns best using his/her eyes. They learn by observing. If given verbal information, it's better from this learner to write it down. During reading, this child may appear to be staring off in space. However, this learner is visualizing the information s/he is reading.

An auditory learner is someone who learns best by listening. This child sounds out words and moves lips when reading. This learner can hear directions and learn from them.

Tactile learners are "hands-on" learners. This learner will remember what he does, not what is seen. When learning to spell, they need to feel the words. Something as simple as allowing this child to use his finger and write the words on the top of his desk will help this child.

A kinesthetic learner likes to move. It is difficult for this learner to stay in a seat. It is hard to keep this child's attention. However, if you let this child move around, s/he will be better focused.

QUESTION:
How am I to meet the needs of all the children if everyone has a different way of learning?

ANSWER:
It's almost impossible to meet everyone's needs at all times. What *is* possible is to include some visual, auditory, kinesthetic, and tactile techniques in each of your lessons. In using all modalities, you will be touching on everyone's learning method.

QUESTION:
How do I determine what a child's learning style is?

ANSWER:
There are learning style inventories that you can administer to children either in a group or individually.

QUESTION:
What if I don't have an inventory?

ANSWER:
Just watch the child. You'll be able to figure out how each child learns. Watch the child especially during play time. Does the child sit and play with puzzles? Then they are tactile and visual learner. Does the child sit and listen to books on tape with a friend? Then they are auditory and visual learners. Does the child enjoy acting out plays, jumping rope, playing basketball? This classifies them as kinesthetic learners. I enjoy guessing the style and then giving the test to see if I'm right.

QUESTION:
Can you give me some examples of how you teach using different learning styles?

ANSWER:S
Two of the hardest areas for me to teach are Social Studies and Science. The reason I find these subjects difficult to teach is that the books are always too difficult for most kids to read on their own. To get around this, I take the following steps to get the material across to them:

• I have the kids sit in a circle or move the desks so that all can see. (Visual)

• I read the Social Studies material directly from the book. (Auditory)

• Students are asked to act out what I am reading. (Kinesthetic)

• After acting out, students gather in groups of four to write out five important facts they learned. (auditory, tactile)

QUESTION:
Can you give another example?

ANSWER:
Yes, let's take a science lesson. You are reading to the children about how plants start from seeds. The seed needs water and sunshine to grow. If it doesn't get enough, it will wilt and die. As you are reading, a child can pretend to be the seed by crouching down. Another child will water the seed by pretending to have a watering can. Then another child will be the sunshine shining down on the seed by spreading out their arms to emit sun rays. The seed will grow and grow and soon become a plant, illustrated by the child who was the seed slowly moving upwards. Then the sun disappears and the child play-

ing the sun leaves the area. No one is around to water the plant and the child with the watering can leaves the area. The plant soon dies, illustrated by the child who is the seed slowly sinking back down to the floor.

In doing this, you have reached the visual learner, auditory learner and kinesthetic learner. When you write about your experiences, you will have reached the tactile learner. Everyone is actively involved. Students are not reading at their desk quietly, or not so quietly.

QUESTION:
Do children have more than one way of learning?

ANSWER:
Yes, you usually have a combination of all of them. For me, I know I am a visual learner. I am not a strong auditory learner. I can remember as a child having books read to me. I would have enjoyed the book much more if I could have read it myself. My mind would wander when anyone read to me.

QUESTION:
What is the best way to teach children?

ANSWER:
I don't know if there is a "best" way. But I do know once children have learned a concept, they will remember it if they teach the learned concept to someone else. I have my first-graders "teach" kindergarten students letter names and sounds. I have my second grade students "teach" my first grade students how to read simple repetitive books. I have my fifth grade students write books and read them to children in younger grades. When you teach someone, you remember 90% of what you have just learned. Compare this to someone who has been lectured on a concept. They remember only 5 %.

Special Education Students

All children should be given the opportunity to succeed in school. Recently, children with special needs have been included in the regular classroom. This has placed an added responsibility on the classroom teacher. I believe the philosophy of having all children learn together is a good one, however administrators must provide classroom teachers with the needed assistance to accomplish this job. Unfortunately, this isn't always done. The task of teaching all children is placed on a classroom teacher who has neither the time nor the skills to accomplish this goal. Below are frequently asked questions about special education students. The procedures mentioned are followed in New York State. You will come away from this chapter with a frame of reference of what needs to be followed, but there may be some variation from state to state.

QUESTION:
What is an IEP?

ANSWER:
An IEP is an acronym for Individualized Educational Plan. An IEP is written by the Committee of Special Education for children who have been identified as in need of special services. As the teacher, you are responsible for following the IEP. Ask the special educational teacher where the IEP is, then read and follow it.

QUESTION:
Who is on the Committee of Special Education (CSE)?

ANSWER:
The Committee consists of the following people:

1. The Special Education Teacher for the child
2. The Director of Special Education who usually is the chairperson for the CSE meeting
3. The Parent Advocate
4. The School Psychologist
5. The parents of the child
6. The regular educational teacher (Classroom teacher)

QUESTION:
What is a Pre-CSE meeting?

ANSWER:
This is where details of the CSE are discussed. The school psychologist and parent advocate do not need to be present at this meeting. Keep in mind parents are encouraged to participate in the writing of the CSE for their child. Therefore, they should be invited to the PRE-CSE and the CSE meeting.

QUESTION:
What does the CSE do? What is its purpose?

ANSWER:
The role of the committee is to formulate a plan of education for the child who is brought before them. They set up realistic objectives and goals for the child. Testing is done to determine a child's strengths and weaknesses. The results of this testing help establish what the child can realistically accomplish for the next school year.

QUESTION:
What if a parent doesn't agree with the results?

ANSWER:
This sometimes happens. A parent can get a private evaluation and bring those results to another CSE meeting.

QUESTION:
What is a triennial?

ANSWER:
Every three years, the psychologist tests special education students and writes out recommendations for this child. These recommendations are given to the special education teacher for help in formulating goals and objectives for this child.

QUESTION:
Are the test results from the psychologist kept in the child's permanent record folder?

ANSWER:
No, I have always had to ask the office personnel to give me the report. All CSE psychological reports are filed together in a separate folder.

QUESTION:
How do you know if a child has had psychological testing completed?

ANSWER:
Sometimes you don't know. If I suspect a report has been done, I'll ask the office personnel to check if a report is in the general file. A report may have been done and the child was not categorized "special education student." Regular education students have psychological tests completed too. If you think your student may have been tested, ask someone at the office to check for you.

QUESTION:
What is the difference between self-contained classrooms and inclusion classrooms?

ANSWER:
A self-contained classroom is where a special education teacher and an aide have their own group of either 6 or 12 children. The difference in the number 6 or 12 children is dependent upon the severity of the needs of the group of children. These child are "self-

contained" in this room and spend the school day with this teacher and aide. The special education teacher is responsible for following the goals and objectives sent forth on the IEP.

If a child is an "inclusion" student, the child is placed in a regular classroom with other students who have IEPs. The special education teacher must follow the goals and objectives by modifying the child's curriculum set forth by the CSE. However, the majority of the teaching time is spent with a regular education teacher.

QUESTION:
What do you mean by "modify the curriculum?"

ANSWER:
Let's suppose the regular education teacher is instructing the whole class about double-digit multiplication and the homework assignment is page 10, problems 11-30. The special education teacher may have her students complete only problems 11-18. Or the special education teacher may have to back up even further and teach single-digit multiplication to her group of students. As the regular education teacher, you need to know what the goals are for this student so that you can modify the curriculum and not frustrate this child.

QUESTION:
Won't I have a special education teacher in my room for the entire day?

ANSWER:
No, the special education teacher has a caseload of students. This caseload may be divided by grade. Therefore, this teacher needs to divide her time between the teachers that are "inclusion" teachers.

QUESTION:
How am I supposed to know which kids have IEP's?

ANSWER:
Usually the Special Education teacher will come to you to let you know which children s/he is responsible for in your room. At that point, ask to see the child's IEP, since you are also responsible for the education of that child.

QUESTION:
I don't feel trained enough to handle some of the problems these children have. What do I do?

ANSWER:
Welcome to the real world of education. All you can do is try your best and explain to your principal, special education teacher, and parent that you are trying your best. There is no easy answer for this question. Someone once said to me, "You never know when the information you have taught will be received and understood by the child." You could teach someone something and four months later, when they are in a different classroom, they get the "aha!" feeling. You'll never know, but you played a part in that child getting the "aha" feeling. To help the child, you can also ask for tips and techniques from the Special Education teacher who is assigned to your room. Also, talk to the Special Education teacher and explain that you need to be aware of all the rules and regulations regarding a special education student. Write down the rules so you'll have them for reference later.

QUESTION:
Is there money available to purchase equipment for children with special needs?

ANSWER:
Usually you have to ask the Director of Special Education for any available money. Explain why you need the purchase you are requesting. For example, if an IEP states a child should listen to someone reading a social studies assignment, you will need a tape recorder and blank tapes to meet this goal. Request it from the Director of Special Education.

QUESTION:
What is an annual review?

ANSWER:
At the end of the school year, the teacher, parents, and the chairperson of the CSE get together and review the goals and objectives for a student. After the goals and objectives are discussed, new goals and objectives are decided upon for the next year. For example, Joey may be receiving speech three times a week and the speech teacher feels Joey can be changed to two times a week. This change has to be agreed upon by all parties.

QUESTION:
What if I don't agree with the new goals and objectives?

ANSWER:
Speak up and say what you think you must for the child. I have always lived by that rule and have never regretted it.

QUESTION:
What if all the goals and objectives for a child are not met? What happens?

ANSWER:
You discuss why those goals were not met and make sure to document your reasons. For example, if a goal was, "Johnny will add double-digits with double-digits with carrying (trading)", and Johnny still can't add single digits ($2 + 3 = 5$). Have *you* contacted the parents about this prior to the meeting? Have *you* documented that you have contacted them? Then *you* have met all of your obligations toward this child.

Sometimes the goals and objectives teachers set are a bit too high. As long as you have proof that you have done what you needed to for this child, you won't have a problem. However, if you haven't documented or contacted parents, you have reason for concern.

QUESTION:
How do I teach 20 regular educational students and 7 special educational students? Don't they all learn at a different rate?

ANSWER:
Yes, they do. That is why it is good to group students according to needs. For example, let's say Joe S. is a special educational student. Joe S. is very good at math, however, he has a difficult time in reading. You could have a general math lesson for everyone, and then give Joe S. a more difficult assignment to do. You might want to have Joe S. help other students in math. It is always a good idea to build the confidences of all children by asking them to teach for you. In reading, you could have a general lesson and give Joe S. an easier book to read. You just need to play around with your teaching style. I have kids do things in groups a lot. In my opinion, kids learn quicker from other kids. There is *no* intimidation factor whatsoever. In addition, it helps with classroom discipline. Even the misbehaved child can help someone learn.

QUESTION:
How do I know if a child needs to be classified as special education?

ANSWER:
That's a tough one to answer without teaching experience. But what I can tell you is that the child who doesn't do well even after you have tried everything you know is probably a candidate for special education. In addition, you could ask a fellow teacher for suggestions on what more you could do for this student. If there are no new suggestions, this child may be a candidate for special education.

QUESTION:
What do I do? What procedure do I use to identify a student?

ANSWER:
This varies from building to building within a district, and definitely from district to district. You usually start with your principal who will tell you the procedure to follow. There is a lot of paperwork that must be done in order to determine if the child is a candidate for special education. For example, a child will be tested by the school psychologist to determine basic strengths and weaknesses. Testing for IQ will also be completed. Talk to your special educational teacher. They know exactly what needs to be done in your particular building.

QUESTION:
Could a medically fragile child be placed in my room?

ANSWER:
Yes, you need to talk with your school nurse about the medical precautions you must know for this child. Also, it is a good idea to be acquainted with CPR procedures, not only for special students, but for all your students.

QUESTION:
The special education teacher comes into my room and the children she services behave inappropriately. How do I handle this?

ANSWER:
If the children seem to act up when the special education teacher appears, you need to do two things. First, talk to your children and tell them their behavior is unacceptable when "Mrs. Jones" comes to help them. Discuss consequences for their inappropriate behavior. That's the easy part. Second, talk to the special education teacher and tell her/him how the children act out when s/he is in the room. Suggest you talk about what you both feel is acceptable behavior. That's the hard part. But you do need to talk with this teacher. Kids know what they can get away with and who they can manipulate.

QUESTION:
Do I have a choice as to whether I have special needs children in my room?

ANSWER:
Usually you don't have a choice. Administrators are free to put children where they feel will be the best educational setting.

How to Help

Students Succeed

Writing and Spelling

Some people feel that in order to write, you need to spell everything correctly. My theory is you learn to write by making mistakes in your spelling along the way.

QUESTION:

My principal wants me to do more writing with my children. Every week I put my penmanship plans in my planbook and every week I'm asked what I am doing in writing.

ANSWER:

Penmanship and writing are two different skills. Penmanship is the ability to form the letters of the alphabet correctly. Writing is the ability to express oneself. Your administrator is looking for writing.

QUESTION:

My kids are in first grade, and they can't write. What do I do?

ANSWER:

I think you may be confusing spelling and writing. They can write, but they may not spell everything correctly.

QUESTION:

How do I get them started in writing?

ANSWER:

Let's suppose you are doing a unit on animals. You might ask the children what their favorite animal is. Then you could ask them to draw their favorite animal. After the drawing, ask them to write about it.

Beginning of First Grade Writing Sample
i hv a k (Student's writing)
I have a cat.

From this little bit of writing, you can tell a lot about a child's development. This child appears to have beginning sounds. The spacing seems appropriate too.

QUESTION:
Should I show this to my administrator with all the misspellings?

ANSWER:
You were asked to show your students' writing. This is what you have , so far. However, by the end of the year, if you keep writing, it will look like the following example.

End of First Grade Writing Sample
I hav a cat.   (or)   I hav a kat.

As you can see, it is getting closer and closer to the correct way of spelling.

QUESTION:
Should I correct the spelling all of the time?

ANSWER:
That depends on what your objective is. If your objective is to get kids writing, just ask them to read what they wrote and applaud them for their efforts. If your objective is to hang up the child's work, then definitely correct everything. It would be helpful if you corrected the paper with the child.

QUESTION:
How do I move beyond one sentence?

ANSWER:
Ask your kids questions. For instance, your conversation may sound like this:

Teacher	You wrote about your cat.
Student	Yeah
Teacher	What is your cat's name?
Student	Spotty
Teacher	How did your cat get that name?
Student	When we first got the cat, it spilled my dad's paint can and got spots all over. My dad wasn't happy, but my mom made a joke out of it and said, "Let's call the cat Spotty."
Teacher	Can you write that all down for me? That's a funny story.
Student	No, I can't spell it all.
Teacher	That's okay, spell the words how they sound. I'll help you when you are all finished.
Student	It's too much to write.
Teacher	It'll make a great story, I want to read it, give it a try.

At this point get up and leave, don't get caught up in disagreeing with the child. Move on to the next student. Even your most reluctant student will try to write a story since you have reassured them that misspellings are okay, and you want to read the story.

QUESTION:
I have too many kids to correct all of those papers. Do I have to?

ANSWER:
Don't correct them. Enjoy their writing for the sole purpose of the student being able to express himself. You don't need to correct everything.

QUESTION:
Aren't my kids writing when they are doing a worksheet that asks them to fill in the blank?

ANSWER:
No, they are just filling in blanks. Let's take a look at one.

Sample of Writing vs Filling in the Blanks

I have a _____ .   dog   the   happy

All the student has to do is take a good guess. They have a pretty good chance of getting the right answer without even thinking.
Now, think about asking a child to write about a dog.

i hv a dg. mi dg is bg.

I have a dog. My dog is big.

When a child is asked to fill in the blanks, there isn't a lot of thinking going on. When a child is asked to put some thoughts on paper, it is more difficult, but more educationally sound.

QUESTION:
I teach second grade. The first grade teacher had the children complete fill in the blank worksheets. Why do I have to do all the writing?

ANSWER:
You have to start the kids writing. Perhaps the first grade teacher wasn't a risk taker, then you need to be. I remember when I first started writing with my kids. I was intimidated by the whole concept. Filling in the blanks was easier. I soon discovered that writing was so much more fun for the children. It also makes more sense educationally.

QUESTION:
Do I have to give my kids a spelling test every week?

ANSWER:
Some schools require a spelling test. Some schools don't. Ask a colleague.

QUESTION:
Where do I get the words for the spelling test?

ANSWER:
Usually you get the words from a spelling book. But if you don't have a book, you can make them up. Just one suggestion, have the words make sense so kids can see the pattern of words. For example, the test may have the following words:

me   he   she   be   we

I have seen kids study the following words:

me   he   go   it   the

For a struggling student, the second list is very difficult because there is no pattern.

QUESTION:
What do you mean by pattern?

ANSWER:
Consonant Vowel Consonant is a pattern. (CVC)

Words such as cat, hat, sat, fat follow the CVC pattern

Words such as cat, hit, set, fit also follow the CVC pattern

Consonant Vowel Consonant e (CVC e) is a pattern

Words such as: make, bite, tape, cute follow the CVC e pattern

QUESTION:
How about longer words? Is there any trick to teaching longer words?

ANSWER:
I teach my kids to spell words by syllables. For example, let's take the word contraction. I would teach them that contraction has three syllables and each syllable must have a vowel. We would draw 3 lines on our paper like this:

_____   _____   _____

We would spell the first syllable, then the second syllable, then the last syllable. We would then circle the vowels, just to reinforce that all syllables must have a vowel.

QUESTION:
How do you teach syllables?

ANSWER:
I used to teach it by clapping out the word. I don't teach it that way anymore because some kids would clap real fast and come up with 4 syllables for the word contraction and some kids would come up with 2 syllables for contraction because they clapped slower.

I learned a technique at a workshop I attended. I hope I am as good at writing out the directions as I am teaching it in front of a group of kids.

1. Let's take the word "contraction"
2. Say the word to yourself and do NOT let the word leave your lips.
3. As you are saying the word, listen in your head for how many parts the word contraction has.

Those are the directions. Try it. It works. I haven't had a child get it wrong using this method.

QUESTION:
When kids are writing, should I help them with words they can't spell?

ANSWER:
I make it a rule, *not* to give the kids the words they ask me to spell. I do guide them though. They know they have to try to spell the word. Let me give you an example. If the word they wanted some help with was 'because', the conversation would go like this:

Student	How do you spell because?
Teacher	How many syllables does it have?
Student	Two syllables
Teacher	Good, draw two lines. What letter does it start with?
Student	I don't know
Teacher	What letter starts the word ball?
Student	B
Teacher	Does B in ball have the same sound as the B in because?
Student	Yes
Teacher	What's the next letter you hear? Buh ee- e- e.
Student	E
Teacher	Yes and there's a vowel for the first syllable
Student	What's next?
Teacher	kuh-kuh-kuh
Student	That's easy, it's a "K"
Teacher	What letter is a copy cat for K?
Student	Oh, I know. It's a C.
Teacher	Yes, and the rest of the word is spelled "ause".

Notice that I guided with part of the word. Some of the letters don't make phonetic sense so I supplied them for the child. If there isn't a sound symbol relationship, don't look for one.

QUESTION:
How about longer words? How do you guide students?

ANSWER:
Let's take the word January. My kids would first draw the lines on their paper for the number of syllables. It would look like this:

_____   _____   _____   _____

I would congratulate them since they got the correct number of syllables.

Their paper may look like this:

<u>Jan</u>   <u>u</u>   <u>air</u>   <u>e</u>

Then, I would ask them to circle the vowels.

<u>Jan</u>   <u>u</u>   <u>air</u>   <u>e</u>

Beneath the syllables they wrote correctly I would make a star. I would gently help them through the incorrect syllables. So the paper would now look like this:

<u>Jan</u>   <u>u</u>   <u>air</u>   <u>e</u>
  *   *

<u>Jan</u>   <u>u</u>   <u>ar</u>   <u>y</u>

I always celebrate what my kids do accurately. It gives them the courage to keep trying. If I had said, "No, that's not how you spell it," I think they would be discouraged. I would also quickly give the child a mini lesson on how "y" sounds like "e".

QUESTION:
Do your kids know the difference between the vowel sounds?

ANSWER:
It depends on the age of the child. Younger students in grades one and two usually don't know the difference. By the end of second grade, most of my kids do know because along with syllabication, I teach them vowel sounds. To me, they go hand in hand. Unfortunately, I also have children in upper grades who don't know the long and short vowel sounds.

QUESTION:
Any tricks in teaching the short and long vowel sounds?

ANSWER:
I learned a trick back in college for the short vowels. As a child I could never remember if "apple" was for "a" or "e". So I taught my kids the way I could remember the short vowel sounds. I told them to imagine they have a dog. The dog's name is Pep short for Pepper. Pep eats and sleeps. So we have the following sentence for Pep:

Fat Pep is not **up**.

Notice the short vowel sounds in each word. If a child tells me they can't remember what short i says, I refer them to the sentence. They quickly give me the correct sound. My room is filled with sentence strips that have 'Fat Pep is not up ' on them. When kids are writing, they will reach for a sentence strip to figure out the sound symbol relationship. I chuckle when I hear the kids say, "Don't ask Mrs. Torreano how to spell a word, she won't tell you unless you try it on your own."

QUESTION:
Do you correct all of their words this way?

ANSWER:
No, only the words that lend themselves to a quick lesson. If I did it to all of the words, they wouldn't listen to me. I always notice the letters they wrote correctly, but I don't always give them a lesson on the letters they wrote incorrectly.

QUESTION:
I have been in primary classes where the teacher has labeled a lot of the room. For example, on her chair, she has Mrs. Torreano. On the desk, she has printed the word desk By the door, there is the word door. What is the reason for this?

ANSWER:
It helps children to see that letters form words and those words stand for something. Some children don't recognize the letters of the alphabet so you have to have the alphabet available. Put words all over. In addition, once children start writing, they will know where to look for words they can't spell. For instance, one of my students was writing a story about me. She spelled my name correctly. I asked her how she figured it out, hoping she'd tell me she sounded it out. She put a big smile on her face and said , "I read your chair. You have your name on it."

QUESTION:
I have a student who is in first grade and is not able to keep up with the other children when it comes to writing or reading. What do I do?

ANSWER:
In every classroom, there will be someone who is having a difficult time keeping up.

As this child's teacher, you need to figure out what the child knows and start from there. For example, I had a student who could not memorize simple word families such as cat, hat, mat, etc. What I needed to do for this student was put my car in reverse and start from what the child knew. I brought the student back to beginning sounds. At first, the child complained and told me it was baby stuff. I convinced this student that since s/he was having a hard time keeping up, I needed to help her/him remember things that had been forgotten. This child is doing wonderful things now. If I didn't put it in reverse, we would both be frustrated. Remember, you need to start a child at their instructional level. You are wasting time teaching things s/he doesn't have the background knowledge for.

QUESTION:
What about older children in grades four through six, who have poor writing skills? How do I help them?

ANSWER:
First, get it clear in your own head what objective you are trying to accomplish. Keep it simple for your sake and their sake. For instance, maybe you want them to just remember to use upper case letters when beginning a sentence, and punctuation marks at the end of a sentence. When correcting their writing, make sure you notice they accomplished the objective you asked for.

QUESTION:
What can I have them write?

ANSWER:
Invite your older students to write simple books for younger students in the building. I am doing this now with my older children and they love it. They can't wait to finish writing and share their books with the young students. What my older students don't know is that I am backing them up and beginning to teach them at their own instructional level. Do my students make many spelling errors? Yes. Do I zero in on them? No. I always have in mind what my objective is and since my objective is upper case letters to begin a sentence and punctuation marks, I don't draw attention to their spelling errors. I always praise them for what they have done correctly. That gives them enough incentive to keep writing since, I don't "red ink" the whole paper.

QUESTION:
How do I begin having my older children write for younger children? I know they'll tell me they don't have anything to write about?

ANSWER:
You're right. They will tell you that. You have to model for them what you are looking for. Have some childrens' books available and show them how the sentences are very short and simple. Show them how the author uses illustrations to convey meaning. Then illicit from them what they can write about. Encourage them to write about what they know about. Guide this part of the lesson carefully. Something like the following:

Teacher	Mary, you told me you enjoy cheerleading. Do you think you could write a book and explain about cheerleading.
Mary	I don't know.
Teacher	What do you know about cheerleading?
Mary	Well, I know we have to do exercises before we do our jumps.
Teacher	I didn't know that. What else?
Mary	Well, we have to work with another friend when we do our jumps.

Teacher   Really? What else do you do?

Mary   Well, we get to go to games and cheer for our team. It's a lot of fun.

Notice the teacher is saying little, but getting the information from the child. At this point, most kids will say I get it, I know what I can write about.

QUESTION:
What about the child who insists he doesn't have anything to write about?

ANSWER:
That child could write about himself. If he tells you he has nothing to write about. Don't back down. Tell him/her to write his name, how many brothers and sisters he has, any pets, etc. This child is probably reluctant to write, but you need to provide a topic that s/he knows about.

QUESTION:
You make it sound easy to get older kids to write, is it?

ANSWER:
I believe it is all in the way you approach writing. If you make it sound exciting, they get excited. Most kids love to play teacher. This is their opportunity to share a book they have written. Once my students start writing, they groan when the timer goes off which signals they have to stop writing. They tell me, "But I was just getting to the good part."

QUESTION:
How do you move from simple sentences to something more challenging with older children?

ANSWER:
Keep your objective simple and keep moving forward. Maybe the next book might require three sentences per page with an emphasis on descriptive words. For example, if a child writes, "I have a dog.", you don't accept it. Tell them to describe their dog. The sentence may now look like this: "I have a beagle with short legs." Keep your objectives small, then look for the objective and congratulate the students who have met the objective.

QUESTION:
What is the "writing process" that I hear teachers talk about?

ANSWER:
People have written good books about the writing process. I'd recommend that you read some of them. The titles have been included in the Reading and Writing References section at the back of this book. I'll try and give you a very *brief* summary. I used the writing process while writing this book. First, I put my thoughts on paper. Then I had friends read my "sloppy copy" and make suggestions as to how I could improve my writing. I then rewrote with their suggestions in mind. Once I finished editing, I gave the book back and had my friends reread my writing.

QUESTION:
That's fine for adults, but what about children?

ANSWER:
The same process is used, but the expectations are not as high with children. Children begin their writing and are told beforehand that the first copy is their "sloppy copy" and it will be corrected and edited.

QUESTION:
What is a "sloppy copy"?

ANSWER:
A "sloppy copy" is the first draft of the writing. Children know they must write on every other line so the person editing their paper has someplace to make suggestions.

QUESTION:
What kinds of suggestions can other children make? Aren't they all about the same level when it comes to writing?

ANSWER:
Basically, yes they are. However , let me be more specific. Let's suppose the following was written by a child:

> I have a new video gam at hom. It is fun. I like it. My mom bout it for me becuz I had a good week at skool. I cant wate to pla it when I get home.

As adults, we see the many spelling errors that this child has made. Some kids will notice them, some kids won't. *Always* know the objective you are trying to teach children. For this example, the objective is *not* spelling, but is content. The conversation with the student would sound like this:

Teacher	Joe, it sounds like you can't wait to get home?
Student	Yeah, my mom bought me a new game.
Teacher	What's the name of the game?
Student	(Student gives name)
Teacher	Who will play the game with you?
Student	I'm going to let my older brother play with me.
Teacher	Where will you be playing the video game?
Student	My mom only lets me play games in the living room. She won't let me play in my bedroom, because sometimes I play longer than what she wants me to play.
Teacher	Joe, can you tell me those things in your writing.
Student	I don't want to, it's too much to write.
Teacher	Joe, it'll make a better story. It's more interesting when you tell me more about it.
Student	Oh, okay, but I don't want to add anymore after that.
Teacher	Okay, write about the name of the game, where you play it, and who you will play with.
Student	(Gives a reluctant OKAY)

Model this conversation in front of the whole class and the kids will understand what they are supposed to look for. After they have completed writing, have children peer conference. You stay out of the conferencing. Kids love to critique other childrens' work.

QUESTION:
What about all the spelling errors? Don't they get corrected?

ANSWER:
Sure they do. But remember, I explained that you need to keep the objective simple. If

the kids think they need to check for content and spelling, they will get all mixed up. Later on, you can expand the conferencing to include spelling, punctuation,etc. But you must also model the appropriate behavior you expect from kids.

QUESTION:
This sound like too much work. What are the benefits of the writing process?

ANSWER:
It is work, but it is also very rewarding. The benefits are many. Children learn to express themselves. Children learn to encourage one another in their writing. Children are more critical of their own writing. The most important benefit I hear is when the timer goes off and kids say, "Do we have to stop? This is fun." You don't hear that when you give them a worksheet to do.

QUESTION:
What if I mess up and don't teach the writing process the correct way?

ANSWER:
Welcome to the club. I made many mistakes as I was learning how to be a "writing workshop" teacher. The kids don't know you are confused. Just fix it. Keep on moving forward. I still make mistakes. I always tell my kids they can make mistakes because I make a lot of mistakes too. They aren't afraid to write and I'm not afraid to keep them writing. Try it, but always know what your objective is. That's where I made my first mistake. I thought the kids had to correct everything.

QUESTION:
What grades have you done writing workshop in?

ANSWER:
I teach reading in kindergarten through fifth grade. Writing workshop is done in grades one through five. A modified version is done in kindergarten.

QUESTION:
Is that all there is to the writing process?

ANSWER:
No, there is a lot more to it. But I wanted to give you a quick lesson. I wanted to give you enough information to be able to try the writing process. You only have enough information to begin. You'll need to read the suggested books in the back to learn more.

Worksheets

You will find that you will need copies of work for your kids in a hurry. What do you do? It's nice to say think ahead, but I know I don't always do. Have some worksheets on hand for the occasional time when you may need them. Also, get to know the copy person in your building and learn how to make copies yourself.

QUESTION:

Do I have to buy my own paper to use with the copy machine?

ANSWER:

I have been in schools where you are given a number limit of paper you can use per year. After your allotment, you have to buy your own paper. I have been in other schools where you can use as much paper as you want. Ask around to find out what the procedure is in your building.

QUESTION:

Are you allowed to copy things out of a book?

ANSWER:

It all depends on the publisher's rights. Look in the book for that information. Some say permission must be given by the publisher and other books say you may copy for your own personal use. Read the fine print.

QUESTION:

The principal doesn't like us to give worksheets to the kids. What do I do? How do I keep the kids busy?

ANSWER:

Ask colleagues what they do instead of worksheets. There are different activities you can do to keep children writing.

You can make centers. For example, a simple deck of cards can serve as a learning center. The directions at that center may be :

1.   Divide the deck in half.
2.   Each student must flip over a card at the same time.

3. When both cards are flipped over, the students must add them together. You can also subtract, multiply, or divide the numbers on the playing cards.

4. The first person to give the correct answer keeps the cards.

5. Count up to see who has the most cards.

6. Use a calculator to check for accuracy.

Whatever you do , make the assignment purposeful. Kids hate to do things they feel are useless. Always have a purpose and explain to the kids what the purpose is.

QUESTION:
Do I have to correct all of the worksheets myself?

ANSWER:
I have had the children correct their own worksheets. I did this for two reasons. One, I wanted to develop a trusting relationship. Also, when something was marked wrong, they could immediately seek out help to find how to do the problem correctly. You will always here, "Mrs. T, he cheated and changed the answer." My reply is, "Who is he hurting?" Usually the offender will quickly mark the answer wrong again.

QUESTION:
Do I let them correct the worksheets all of the time?

ANSWER:
No. If you are trying to see if children *understood* a concept you have taught, then go ahead and let them correct it. If you are *testing* a concept, then you should correct this worksheet yourself.

QUESTION:
How often should I give children worksheets?

ANSWER:
That depends on your teaching style. I enjoy having the children engaged in whatever they are doing. I also don't mind noise, some teachers do mind the noise. Figure out what your teaching style is and then you 'll know if you want to use worksheets or not.

QUESTION:
What can I do with the kids besides giving them worksheets?

ANSWER:
Let's suppose you want to test their understanding of multiplication of single-digit numbers. Besides giving them a worksheet, you could:

1. Have them make a worksheet with ten problems and give the worksheet to a friend. The child who made the worksheet can then correct it and hand it to you. Kids love to play teacher.

2. You could give the children a deck of playing cards with the numbers 1–9, if you are teaching all facts. This game would be played with two children. The children can each flip one card over and multiply the numbers on the cards together. To check for accuracy of their answer, give them a calculator. They are not only learning their multiplication facts, but they are also learning how to use a calculator.

3. Give them multiplication flash cards they can play with in a corner of the room.

Do you notice that children are covering the concept of multiplication? All but the first example do not involve a worksheet.

QUESTION:

What about learning beginning sounds? I have a lot of worksheets where the children have to circle the picture of the letter that matches the sound. What else could I do?

ANSWER:

You could have the children look through magazines and make a poster with "B" words. You could have the children look through books and write down the words that begin with the letter "B". They may not be able to read the words, but that's okay. They are associating the fact that letters make up words. In both of these activities, the children can work with a partner. This is referred to as Cooperative Learning. Worksheets are okay to use on occasion, but when you use them as a steady diet, kids get restless and bored and make mistakes.

QUESTION:

What about testing a child's knowledge about an explorer? Doesn't a worksheet make sense?

ANSWER:

There are other ways to find out the same information. Why not have the children come up with questions about the explorer *and* the answers to their own questions. In doing this, you will know the depth of what they understand. I usually have the kids fold their papers in half horizontally, and then again the same way. They are to write out the question and answer in the space provided by their folds. After I have read them, I cut them up and we play a game of tic-tac-toe with their questions. The kids are highly motivated. They can't wait to hear their question read to see if they have stumped any of their classmates. Here again, no worksheet, but I found out what kids know.

Testing

Testing is a necessary component of school life. There is periodic testing for knowledge on the curriculum you teach, and there is standardized testing which usually occurs at the end of the year. This chapter will discuss both types of testing.

QUESTION:
How often do I have to test children in the subject areas of reading, math, social studies, and science?

ANSWER:
Usually it is wise to test after a specific concept has been taught. For example, if you are teaching single-digit addition and will be moving on to double-digit addition, you may need to test the single-digit addition before you move on to double-digit. In the content areas of social studies and science, look at how the chapter is divided and you will be able to determine when to give a test of understanding. Usually publishers have tests already made for each chapter. For reading, publishers have unit/theme tests after a certain amount of stories are read. These tests are supplied by the publisher.

QUESTION:
Should I ever test before teaching a concept?

ANSWER:
Sure, you could use the test to determine whether or not your students need to learn a concept. For example, let's suppose you were beginning a unit on single-digit multiplication. If you tested your students on multiplication, you would be able to determine whether or not all students needed teaching, reteaching, or were ready to move on to double-digit times single-digit multiplication. Pretesting is a quick way to determine childrens' needs.

QUESTION:
How many questions should I ask on a pretest?

ANSWER:
Keep it short. You could ask ten questions. First, however, explain to the children what a pretest is. They need to know they aren't expected to know the answers.

QUESTION:
Do I have to put all of the grades in my grade book?

ANSWER:

That is up to you. If many of your children fail your test, you may want to reteach and then test again. Your grade book entry could look like this–67/87. The first number being the first time you gave the test, the second number being the second time you gave the test.

QUESTION:

Why would I want to put in both grades?

ANSWER:

You could show parents what happens when children study for a test, if that is the problem. Or you could have a reminder for yourself that a particular concept has proven to be difficult for the majority of the students. When you teach that concept the following year, you may decide that you have to do something different.

QUESTION:

How many grades do I have to put in my grade book?

ANSWER:

Different schools work have certain expectations. Some schools want one grade per subject per week. Some schools want two grades for reading, math, language arts, but only one grade for social and science. You could ask your principal what the expectations are or ask a colleague.

QUESTION:

If all the students fail my test, can I eliminate that grade in the grade book?

ANSWER:

Sure. What you put in your grade book is up to you. You should not penalize a student for something that needs to be retaught. If most of your children failed the test, it's probably due to the fact the concept needs to be retaught in a different way. Perhaps more hands-on materials are needed for that particular concept.

QUESTION:

Should any of my test papers be sent home?

ANSWER:

I would recommend that you send home any major test paper for a parent signature. Date the paper with your date stamper. When the paper is returned, file it and keep it. You may need the papers if you are thinking of retaining a child or putting in a referral for a child. Also, do *not* throw the papers out until the beginning of the next school year. You need to do this because if, in the following year, a parent doesn't agree with your recommendation, they may decide to go over your head. Sometimes parents don't complain until the following school year. You will need documentation as to why you repeated that child. I know a teacher who went looking in the dumpster for a child's papers she mistakingly threw out at the end of the year. Keep all papers until the dust settles in the new school year.

QUESTION:

How do I figure out final ten week averages? I have grades for homework, tests, and daily papers.

ANSWER:

Figure out how much weight you want to put on each type of assignment. For example, you may want to count a final test as two grades and homework as only one grade. You need to figure out how much weight you want to give to each item. Let's assume your grade book looks like this:

Math	1 digit multipl.	2 digit multipli.	Test	Homework
	85%	75%	88%	65%

You may want to calculate the average by counting the *test* grade twice. So your final average would be 80% (85 + 75 + 88 + 88 + 65 divided by 5). You can also ask a colleague in the same grade how to figure out 10 week-averages.

QUESTION:
Some of the textbooks have tests already made up. Do I have to use them?

ANSWER:
No, you can use whatever you want. Some teachers use the publisher's tests as a pretest and then make up their own post test. What you use is up to you, as long as your test reflects the material you have covered. You could also have the children come up with test questions. They would start their questions using the words Who, What, Where, When and Why. By making up questions, the kids are already reviewing for the test.

QUESTION:
What are standardized tests?

ANSWER:
Standardized tests are tests that are given state wide or country-wide. The test results are given in percentile and stanine scores. Boards of Education and administrators look at these results to see how your school is doing as a group. They also look to see how your class is doing. Unfortunately, they are also used to compare your school district with other school districts.

QUESTION:
How do I read the results? What is a stanine?

ANSWER:
A stanine is a measurement, just like an inch is a measurement. Stanines are numbered 1–9. If a student falls between the 4th, 5th and 6th stanine, they are considered an average student. If a student scores in the 7th, 8th, or 9th stanine, they are considered above average. If a student falls below the 4th stanine, they are considered below average.

QUESTION:
What about percentile? If a student scores a 99, does that mean he got a 99 on the test?

ANSWER:
No, it means he scored better than 99% of 100 people tested at his grade level.

QUESTION:
When are standardized tests given?

ANSWER:
That varies school to school. In New York state, our school year ends in June. Most of New York state's standardized tests are given in May. Teachers have the results by June.

QUESTION:
What if a student is having a bad day? Won't that reflect on his test?

ANSWER:
It sure does reflect on the results. Unfortunately, the test doesn't take into effect childrens' emotional variability.

QUESTION:
Does my administrator look at my test results for my class?

ANSWER:
Yes, your administrator will look at test results. Let's suppose your results are not good in math. An administrator may ask you how you are teaching math. They may offer some advice on how to raise your test scores. Bad test results reflect not only on you, but on your administrator.

QUESTION:
Doesn't that put a lot of pressure on teachers for one test?

ANSWER:
Yes, but I've been teaching for over 24 years and there has been no change in test pressure. When it is over, the children and the teachers breathe a sigh of relief.

Reading

As a classroom teacher from 1975-1979, and a reading teacher
since 1979, I have watched different reading theories come and
go. In order to teach children to read, you have to provide them
with the necessary tools. This chapter explains what I feel are
the necessary tools and how to teach those tools to children.
Keep in mind, this is my theory. But also keep in mind, I know it
works!

QUESTION:
It's the first week of school. How do I group my students for reading lessons?

ANSWER:
Don't worry about grouping the first week. You will learn about your childrens' strengths and weaknesses as you teach them. In the beginning, you will probably use whole group instruction and branch off once you determine your students' needs. You will find those handful of children that are way beyond what you are doing and you can give them materials to meet their needs. You will also find those children that are way below your instruction and you will have to find ways to meet their needs too.

Let's suppose you teach first grade. You can go over the concepts that should have been mastered in kindergarten and you will soon see who has or hasn't mastered these concepts. You may want to get a writing sample from each child. This is very simple to do, but they will tell you, "I can't write." What they are really saying is , "I can't spell." Tell them to spell everything as best as they can. Through their writing, you will be able to analyze what their needs are.

Have them draw a picture about their favorite place to visit, or favorite toy, or what they did when their friend stayed at their house. Have them try to draw, and then have them write about their drawing. They will complain, but have them write anyway. You will begin to see by their writing what they need. Do their letters run all together as if there are no separate words? (i.e. Iwantadg) Do they leave spaces between their words? (i.e. My nameis Mary,whatis your name) What about punctuation? What about upper case or lower case letters or is their writing a mixture of both? (i.e. i WAnT a NEw ToY.)

You'll be able to group your children by observing them the first week. Do not put pressure on yourself to immediately meet everyone's needs. It is impossible!

The hardest lesson I have to learn, and I learn it every year, is that with beginning readers it takes time for them to learn how to read. Give the kids and yourself time to enjoy the process. There are children that come to me on September 1st and I am frustrated by September 22nd because they aren't reading. I am being unrealistic. My expectations are way off. My first graders begin to read by November or December. But, then they fly! Hang in there first grade teachers, your kids have a lot to memorize before they can read.

Teachers of students in second through third grade, you can also observe during the first week. You will be able to learn a lot through your own eyes. Take your time before you put children in a group. If you have made a mistake and placed children in the wrong group, correct it.

For older students in grades four and five, the same principle applies. Don't worry about grouping the first week. Observe children. Give them 20 minutes of silent reading time. Pay attention to the type of book they select. Is it a picture book? Is it a chapter book? Ask them to read you a few sentences. Can they read it? By listening to a child read, you will be able to hear if the book is on the appropriate level. Listen to a child privately so as not to embarrass a child who is having a difficult time reading.

Have the children write for you. Take a look at this sample from a fourth grade student:

> I hav a dog at home he is vere nise. i like him because he plas with
>
> me he tryed to bite mi sister and i lafed. My mom got mad at me? i
>
> had to go to mi rom.

Can you identify this child's strengths and weaknesses? Praise the child's strengths and teach this child *one* of the weaknesses. Maybe all you want to do is teach how to write the word "I". Expect to see the word "I" correctly written in all subsequent writings. When you do see the child writing it correctly, praise the child.

QUESTION:
How do I group? What do I base my groupings on?

ANSWER:
You base your groups on needs of the children and those needs will vary. It is called "flexible grouping." For example, you may have students who can alphabetize up to the second letter and students who aren't sure what A-B-C order means. You will group children according to their specific need.

Another example, you may have children who can read a graph for literal information, but are unable to interpret that information. Other children may be able to do both. You would group again according to need. Based on your findings, you can have children teach other children. It's a great strategy that helps everyone.

QUESTION:
I'm a first grade teacher and some of my students don't know the alphabet yet, what do I do?

ANSWER:
Unfortunately, this does happen. You must give your students the basics they have somehow missed. Invite the parents in for a conference to discuss their child's needs. If the parents don't come in, document this. Move on to the next step, and illicit help from an older student in the building. Have an older child responsible for going over alphabet flash cards with a student who does not know the alphabet.

Instead of reviewing all 26 letters, just do 4 or 5 letters at a time. Do not do "b" along with "d" or "p" along with "q". These are too confusing for students. Once your first grade student can identify four or five letters, have him find those letters in old magazines and circle them. Your first-grader doesn't have to read those words to you, but eventually they will get the idea that letters form words. Keep increasing the number of letters you want this child to learn until they have mastered all 26. This will take some time. I always get frustrated when the child "forgets", but in order to remember something, you must see it quite a few times. If you are the only one exposing this child to the letters, it may take a while.

Another strategy to help a child remember the letters is to play a game of memory. (See Games Appendix for directions on how to play Memory) Don't play with all 26 letters. It will be very frustrating for the first-grader to try and remember where all 26 letters are.

QUESTION:
Should I teach my students phonics?

ANSWER:
I have always been a firm believer in phonics. When different reading theories were circulating, I listened and learned, but I always taught my students phonics. How you teach phonics is up to you. Regardless of method, I think it is very important to teach phonics. I think of phonics as the roots to a tree. If the tree didn't have roots, it wouldn't grow. If your students don't have phonics, they will wilt and no amount of water is going to bring them back. They need phonics to provide the roots of decoding. There are people that disagree with me, but in all my years of teaching I am proud to say I have always been able to teach a child to read. You guessed it, they have all been taught phonics.

QUESTION:
Should I use a phonics books to teach phonics?

ANSWER:
That is entirely up to you. When I started teaching, I used a phonics book. I needed some sort of prepared sequence. Now, I teach phonics using a student's own words. For example, my kids might write the following:

> I hv a dg at hom. (I have a dog at home.)

I would correct some of the mistakes together with the child. Our conversation may sound like this:

Teacher	I like the way you started your sentence with a capital letter. Do you know what letter comes after the H in have?
Student	No.
Teacher	Would it be an "A" as in fat or an "U" as in up?
Student	I don't know.
Teacher	It would be an "A" as in fat .
Student	Oh.
Teacher	There's an " E" at the end of the word. Let's just put it down.
Student	OK.
Teacher	I like the way you spelled dog. That letter "O" is hard to hear. Dog is spelled d—o—g.
Student	OK.
Teacher	Do you remember what we learned about long vowels? Sometimes there

is a letter at the end to help make the vowel long or make the vowel say its name.

Student   YES, magic "E".

Teacher   There you go, home is h—o—m—e.

Notice, this was a phonics lesson that did not involve a worksheet, but the student learned using his own words. This can be done over and over again. Always celebrate what the child did correctly and gently help them where help is needed.

QUESTION:
Are you saying I should never use worksheets to teach phonics?

ANSWER:
No, I am saying that you might want to limit the use of worksheets. Whatever concept you are covering in class, *expect* to see it correctly in their writing. Or expect to remind the student that it is something that has been covered before.

QUESTION:
I teach third grade and some of my kids can read very well and some kids struggle over the simplest books. Any ideas?

ANSWER:
This idea may work, but it is highly dependent on the kinds of kids you have. You could have your better reader "Peer Read" with your struggling students. Peer Reading is when two students share the same book and your better reader helps the struggling student read the book. Ground rules must be set before hand. By that I mean you must explain to the students that we are here to help each other. Model what is acceptable. Pretend you are a struggling student and show the class how you would help that person. Usually kids love to help other kids, but as I said this is highly dependent on the types of students you have.

QUESTION:
How do I teach reading along with social studies, science, math and all the other subjects I am required to teach?

ANSWER:
It is hard to do it all, but it isn't impossible. You can teach the content areas (social studies and science) and reading at the same time. As their teacher, you want your children to understand the concepts of what you are teaching. For example, let's suppose you are teaching a lesson on plants in science. You can find in your local library a book on plants and read that book to your children. Before reading the book , ask the children what they already know about plants and write those facts on the board. This method is called K-W-L Strategy.

Sample K-W-L Format		
Know	What they want to know	Learn

Then, illicit from the students what they would like to know. Accept all of their answers. Finally, after reading the book on plants, illicit from the students what they have learned. In doing this, you have set a purpose for reading. Many times children don't know what to listen for. This is sort of a "guide as your read approach."

In the beginning you can do a K-W-L together. Later students can do this on their own. Try it. It works!

QUESTION:
That sounds like a good approach, but the child didn't read the text.

ANSWER:
You're right. However, when the child reads it, s/he will know how to read for the meaning in the content areas. Many children can read fiction, but have a difficult time understanding non-fiction.

QUESTION:
I have students who have little or no interest in reading. What can I do for them?

ANSWER:
They probably have no interest in reading because they find reading difficult . What you can do is simplify reading for them. Instead of the student having to read, have the student listen to books and follow along as the voice on the tape reads to them. Get a book that is way below the child's level so the child will meet with success. S/He may tell you, "That's too easy." I answer with, "No, it isn't easy, you are just getting smarter."

QUESTION:
Where do I find read-a-long books?

ANSWER:
Students usually get book orders from major publishers. You can find read-a-long books in the book order. In addition, the books should be free to you. How? You calculate how many books your children order and you get so many points for the order. You can use those points to buy books from the publisher. During my first year of teaching , I used all of my points to stock my room with books I wanted for the children. I also put my name on those books so I'd be able to easily locate my books to take with me if I left the school to teach elsewhere.

QUESTION:
How often should I send the book orders home?

ANSWER:
Usually, once every four to five weeks is sufficient. Encourage parents to make a check out to the company for the exact amount of their child's order. Ask them to put the order blank and check in a separate envelope with their child's name clearly printed. Ask parents not to put in money, since money tends to get lost.

QUESTION:
Could I encourage parents to buy a particular book if I want to use it in school for a lesson?

ANSWER:
I know it has been done. But I would check with your administrator to make sure there won't be a problem. You can encourage parents to purchase a particular book. With the children who don't get the book, you can use your free bonus points to get additional copies.

QUESTION:
Our library has a lot of books, but doesn't have multiple copies. Is there anything I can do about that?

ANSWER:
You can try talking to your librarian and give suggestions of books you would like to have multiple copies of. Sometimes the librarian doesn't know you want a particular book. I have found that when I request something and provide a reason why, I usually get what I want.

QUESTION:
What do you mean when you say children need to model reading for each other?

ANSWER:
In a classroom setting, there will be diverse ability levels in all subject areas. It is usually quickly evident in reading. Once you know your better readers, it is a good idea to pair them with your struggling readers. Have your better readers *read* to the struggling readers. They will be modeling reading the way it should be done. Kids strive to be like other kids and this will encourage them to be better readers.

QUESTION:
Won't the struggling readers be frustrated listening to someone who can read better than they can?

ANSWER:
Kids usually enjoy being with other kids and they will strive to do their best for another child. If you can keep the same kids paired together, you will see that the struggling reader will become less dependent on the better reader. You need to provide reading material that the struggling reader can read independently. Sometimes you have to dig around to find the right book.

QUESTION:
How do I get my kids to memorize high frequency words? Some of the words are not phonetic, so I can't tell them to sound them out.

ANSWER:
Some of the words that are high frequency need to be seen over and over again. One tool that I use is a word ring. I buy index cards and a three and a half inch book ring to put the words on. Initially , I give the students three words to learn . If the student can say the word correctly, s/he gets a star. As soon as they get five stars, I tell them the word now belongs to them. I build on their book ring once a week. The next time, I may give them four words. Now they have a total of seven. By the end of the year, they love to count how many words they know.

QUESTION:
How do you keep track of when they got their new words?

ANSWER:
I use the date stamper that I bought at the grocery store. Usually I let the kids stamp their own words. They love to do it.

QUESTION:
Don't word rings get lost?

ANSWER:
Yes, all the time. I have found a solution to that. When a student has to copy all of the words over again on his own, they seem to take better care of the word ring.

QUESTION:
How do you keep track of who gets what words?

ANSWER:
I have a list of words. I also have index cards with each child's name on it that I have in my file folder. Let's suppose Mary received the words."the", "said", and "with".

On Mary's index card, I would have stamped the date and written the word "with". To me that means Mary has all of the words up to "with". It saves me time from writing all of the words down.

QUESTION:
What does the whole file folder look like?

ANSWER:
Here's a sample of what it looks like:

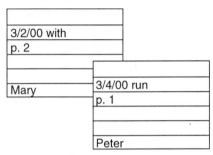

QUESTION:
Do the kids really study the words?

ANSWER:
In the beginning, yes, they do study. Then I need to make phone calls home to stress to parents to look for the word ring and my purpose in giving the child the word ring.

QUESTION:
I have 26 kids in my room. It seem impossible to give them all word rings.

ANSWER:
I am responsible for approximately 40 children. I don't give word rings to all of them. Give word rings only to the children who are struggling. The only way I keep track of students and their words is by using the index cards that I keep in a regular file folder.

QUESTION:
Any tricks for helping children read social studies and science books? They always seem so difficult for the kids.

ANSWER:
Unfortunately, content books are usually not on a child's instructional level due to the vocabulary . Always set a purpose for reading. For example, you could change the heading into a question. Let's presume the heading is *Communication*. On a sheet of paper students will have written the following:

Who What Where When Why and How

Then ask them to write out questions about the topic. For example, under "What"— What is communication? Next to "When"—When do people communicate? Next to "Why"—Why do people communicate? Students do not need to use all of the words, but they do need to formulate questions around the topic heading. This sets a purpose for their reading. Then after reading, have them answer their own questions. They can do this orally or in writing.

QUESTION:
My kids read their social studies book and proudly announce after five minutes that they are finished reading. When I ask them what they have read I hear , "I dunno". Will writing out the "who, what, where, when , why and how" questions help them?

ANSWER:
Yes it will, because now they have a purpose for reading.

QUESTION:
What if a child can't read to use this technique?

ANSWER:
Have another child read with the struggling reader and make them both responsible for the questions using Who , What, Where, When , Why and How.

QUESTION:
Any other ideas to help children with the content area?

ANSWER:
I use pantomime. I read the material and I have a few kids act out what I am reading. Everyone pays attention because it is a lot of fun.

QUESTION:
My students have many words they need to memorize the meaning for and they can't even read the words. Any suggestions?

ANSWER:
You might want to try the following method. Have a child fold a paper in quarters. In the bottom left section, write the word the child needs to memorize. For example, the word transportation may be written there. Then, in the same block, have the child draw a picture of what transportation means. Finally, ask the child why he drew that particular picture. You'll hear, "Transportation is a way of getting from place to place and my car takes us places. My dad left for a trip and we took him to the airport in our car."

By using pictures to memorize a vocabulary word, the child will remember the word easier. Do the same for any word you want a child to memorize.

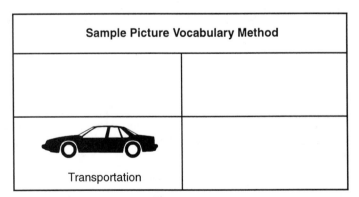

Sample Picture Vocabulary Method	
Transportation	

My eigth grade son still uses the picture vocabulary method I taught him when he was younger. His comment to me, "Mom, this really works."

QUESTION:
Why not have the child memorize the word and its meaning?

ANSWER:
Pictures seem to be easier to memorize than words.

QUESTION:
Why did you fold the paper in quarters?

ANSWER:
After the student has drawn four different pictures, you could cut the pictures and use them as flash card study helpers.

QUESTION:
Does this method work?

ANSWER:
Yes, it does work. I had a student staring out the window during a test. The question was about communication. The student saw telephone wires and remembered he had drawn wires on his paper for communication. He was able to define communication correctly.

QUESTION:
What is the most important thing a teacher could do to encourage a student to read?

ANSWER:
Find quality literature and read to them daily. You might want to stop at a "good part" and invite the students to read more on their own. You'll usually see kids grab for that book later on if you have silent reading time built into your schedule.

Children's Books

There are many different children's books on the market today. The books I am suggesting are books I am using with my students. However, there are many more wonderful titles. You will need to go to a bookstore and browse.

QUESTION:
What books should I use with my younger children? (Grades K-3)

ANSWER:
That all depends upon the purpose for using the book. If you want a book for pure enjoyment, read the book yourself and determine if it's enjoyable. If the book is to teach a particular objective, read the book and see if your objective can be met using that book.

QUESTION:
Is it worthwhile to sit and read to children?

ANSWER:
YES!!! Reading books to children should be done every day. You could read a short book or get a chapter book. Both have their own merits.

QUESTION:
What are the merits of chapter books and books that can be read at one sitting?

ANSWER:
If you read students a chapter book and stop at an exciting part, you will find some children who take the book off your desk and read to find out "what happens." This is exactly what you want. One goal you should try and reach is to encourage more reading for all your students. If you read a short book, children may pick it up to read because they'll want to read it on their own. I used both types of children's books.

QUESTION:
Can you recommend any particular authors?

ANSWER:
I can, but keep in mind I am only scratching the surface. For younger children (Grades K-3) you may want to try the following authors:

1. Tomie de Paolo
2. Frank Asch
3. Eric Carle
4. Marc Brown

5. Mercer Mayer
6. Cynthia Rylant
7. Arnold Lobel
8. Marjorie Weinman Sharmat

QUESTION:
What about older children (Grades 4-6)?

ANSWER:
A popular series for them is The Magic School Bus Series. The author is Joanna Cole. She has a wonderful way of teaching social studies and science concepts using her Magic Bus. The kids love it and understand the concept. I would highly recommend using her books. Another author is R. Dahl. Girls enjoy the American Girl Series by Valerie Tripp. You may also want to try Suzy Kline who writes about Horrible Harry.

QUESTION:
What about children who refuse to pick up a book because they have a difficult time reading?

ANSWER:
You may want to offer them books on tape. This is a great alternative. Most book orders have books on tape. If possible, order enough copies for your entire class. If not possible, just order one. The children love following along while someone is reading to them.

QUESTION:
What is D. E. A. R. time?

ANSWER:
D. E. A. R. is Drop Everything And Read. Some schools recommend that part of your day be spent with D. E. A. R. time. Some teachers have D. E. A. R. right after lunch. It calms everyone down. Everyone, including the teacher spends 10–15 minutes reading.

QUESTION:
What about the child who doesn't have a book for D. E. A. R.?

ANSWER:
You should try and have books in your classroom on all levels so that all children can have a book. It could also be a magazine. It could even be the newspaper. It doesn't matter what they read as long as they read.

QUESTION:
Any precautions I need to be aware of with books?

ANSWER
Yes, if you are planning on reading a book to your class, make sure you read it first. Sometimes authors write things which I feel are inappropriate. To avoid any embarrassment or parent complaints, read the book first and use your own judgment.

QUESTION:
Any other recommendations?

ANSWER:
The most important thing to do is make sure you do read to your class. Some teachers read right before the buses. Children are all ready to go home and this calms everyone down. It doesn't matter when you read, it only matters THAT you read.

Homework

Some teachers give homework, some teachers don't give home-work. If you decide to give homework, make it purposeful. I have seen too many children that come home with purposeless home-work. I would think their time would be better spent running around outside and getting some exercise.

QUESTION:
Do I have to give homework?

ANSWER:
Your school may have a policy on homework. Find out if there is such a policy. One school I worked at insisted upon at least 15 minutes per day. Another school left it up to the teacher.

QUESTION:
Should I give homework every night?

ANSWER:
You may have a building policy on homework, but if you don't, I would suggest giving homework only a few days a week. I would leave weekends "homework free." I would recommend that your children read every night before bed. It could be a magazine, or comics, it doesn't have to be a book.

QUESTION:
Why should I give homework?

ANSWER:
Good question! In my opinion homework should be given for a purpose and that pur-pose should be *review* of material. I would not give homework on a new concept. It isn't fair to the children or the parents who try to figure out the assignment.

QUESTION:
How long should I expect children to spend on their homework?

ANSWER:
I know a teacher who told parents that a child should spend only 15–20 minutes on homework. After that, the paper gets signed by the parent and noted that Johnny spent 20 minutes on this paper. I thought that was a good idea. If it takes a child longer to do

an assignment, they probably don't understand it. It would then be your job to reteach that concept.

QUESTION:
Should I have parents help with homework?

ANSWER:
That's up to you. It would help if you told the children to have their parents sign the paper if they did help. By signing, you could see who was actively involved in their child's education.

QUESTION:
I have a student who consistently fails his open book social studies and science quizzes. But if I give an open book quiz for homework, the student passes. How do I grade something I think a student is getting help with?

ANSWER:
You would first have to start by asking the student who helped with the homework. Usually kids will tell you, "My mom or my brother helped me." It will be up to you to find out just how much "Help" the child received. You may want to call the parent to find out what happened with the homework. I have had parents tell me that the older brother did the entire assignment. At that point, you'll have to explain to the parent what your expectations are. Most parents will want some advice, especially if they genuinely want to help their child.

QUESTION:
Should I grade homework and put the mark in my class grade book?

ANSWER:
This is up to you. Some teachers tell kids they are going to look to make sure it is completed. There would be no grade. Other teachers tell students homework will be graded, but won't tell them which homework assignment will be graded. I don't like to grade homework because I'm never sure who is really getting the grade. Is it the child, the child's parent, or the child's brother or sister? I *always* check to make sure it is completed, but I don't attach any grade to it.

QUESTION:
Don't the kids get sloppy if they know it isn't going to be graded?

ANSWER:
Yes, and if it is too sloppy, they have to do the entire paper over again. If that happens, they are very careful about their work.

QUESTION:
I have a child who consistently doesn't hand in homework. What do I do?

ANSWER:
You can start by taking away any free time you may offer the kids. Maybe you have a quick game you play with the class. This can also be taken away from the student who doesn't complete the homework. When kids are playing, the child who missed the homework is making up the work. You can also telephone home and explain to the parents what is going on. Usually, you will get support from parents. On the occasion that you don't get support from parents, you are on your own as far as consequences. Find out what the child likes and take it away until the homework is done consistently.

QUESTION:
How do I make sure the homework gets home?

ANSWER:

In the beginning of the school year, give the children folders with pockets. Before buses come, have them take out their "Go Home Folder". This folder will contain any notes that parents must see, and homework. Walk around the room and make sure the children have their homework in the folder. Once a week, you may want to clean up the "Go Home Folder." You'll find notes nestled between the folds of the folder that should have gone home, but didn't.

QUESTION:

Where do I get 25 pocket folders?

ANSWER:

In the beginning of the year, you can give children a supply list. Include this item on your supply list. For the following school year, include this item on *your* supply list. Keep it on the child's supply list, but you will have some students who can't afford or forget to bring the folder in. Now you will have a folder to give them.

Games

Children love to play games. I use popular games they enjoy and put an educational twist to them. Here are a few of the games I use with my students. Be creative, watch kids play, then make that game educational. More games can be found in the Games Appendix at the back of this book.

QUESTION:
How do I make learning interesting for the kids?

ANSWER:
My kids love to play Tic-Tac-Toe. So whatever the assignment, I play Tic-Tac-Toe with them. Let's say they are studying long vowel words. I would put long vowel words in a Tic-Tac-Toe diagram. Divide the kids into two teams. The kids take turns saying the words. If they are correct, they put an X or an O on the diagram.

Sample Tic-Tac-Toe Board		
Team A "X"	Team B "O"	
boat	hide	made
home	size	make
bone	cave	rude

You could also use the Tic-Tac-Toe board for comprehension. Ask a question, if the child gets the correct answer, s/he puts an X or an O in the space.

QUESTION:
Any other games?

ANSWER:
Yes, I have played "To Tell The Truth" with older children. This is a bit tricky. Three students are with me out in the hall for a few seconds. I tell one of them that s/he must

always tell the truth. If s/he doesn't know the answer to a question, s/he may respond with , "I don't know." The other two students can answer correctly some of the time, but need to also answer some questions incorrectly. The other classmates need to identify the person who is *always* telling the truth. Let me be a little specific.

Person 1 Tells the truth	Person 2 Doesn't tell the truth	Person 3 Doesn't tell the truth
Student	How do you spell *contraction* Person 1?	
Person 1	c o n t r a c t i o n	
Student	How do you spell *Maryland* Person 2?	
Person 2	M a r y l a n e	
Student	Person 2, how do you spell *truth*?	
Person 2	T r u t h	
Student	How do you spell *people* Person 1	
Person 1	I don't know	

Note that Person 2 can tell the truth some of the time. It is up to the students to figure out who is telling the truth all of the time.

This game keeps everyone on their toes. You can use the same concept for asking questions in the content area. When you feel enough questions have been asked, you have the rest of the class vote. They can vote using paper or through the use of their fingers. They can hold up 1 finger for Person 1, 2 fingers for Person 2, and 3 fingers for Person 3.

QUESTION:
Any other ideas?

ANSWER:
What about Checkers? Kids love to play Checkers. Make a Checkers worksheet and put vocabulary words on the squares. In order to take a square, they have to say the word correctly. You could put math computation on the squares too. Use your imagination, you'll be able to come up with many ideas for this popular game.

QUESTION:
Any other?

ANSWER:
Do you have a timer in your room? Set it for three minutes. Have the children write as many words as they can think of that relate to the study of plants you are learning about in science. They could write the names of the states in the United States for three minutes. You will be surprised at the number of kids who can only come up with the city they live in.

QUESTION:
I'd love to play games, but my kids are rude to each other if they don't win. What do I do?

ANSWER:
After all games, I line the kids up on two sides and we shake hands just like they do in soccer or any other sport. While shaking hands, they are asked to say "Good Game." Sometimes I will hear a student say "Bad Game". If that happens, that student does not play the next game.

QUESTION:
I have kids that have to be moving all the time. What game can I play with them?

ANSWER:
I have played Tic-Tac-Toe by putting masking tape on the floor in the shape of the Tic-Tac-Toe board. I make cards with X and O on them. If a child gets the correct answer, the child holds the X or O card in the square of their choice. It keeps them up and moving.

QUESTION:
What can I do with dice?

ANSWER:
One suggestion is use the dice for spelling games. Two children work together. One child rolls the dice. Add up the amounts. The other child rolls the dice. Add up the amounts. Whoever has the largest total gets to be the teacher and asks the other child how to spell a word. After a pre determined amount of time, count up the number of spelling words a child has. The child with the largest amount of words is the winner. Both children are studying spelling words. The teacher is looking at the words and the child writing is paying attention to the written word.

QUESTION:
Any other game ideas?

ANSWER:
Watch your kids play. See what they enjoy doing and put an educational twist to it. What could you do with Jump Rope, Four Corners, Mumball, etc?

FIELD TRIPS

Field trips are educational trips you take with your class. Some schools allow one field trip per class. Some teachers take a field trip with another class so they can double up and have two per year.

QUESTION:
How do I know if I can take my students to a particular place for a field trip?

ANSWER:
Generally, if you have an educational purpose for the place you are planning on taking them, you are permitted to go. For example, some students went to a grocery store. What was the purpose of this trip? To learn about pricing and how to read the price labels for comparative shopping. Also, they learned about categorizing and how soaps are displayed together, bread items are displayed together, etc.

I recently took my class to a local cable television station. The children wrote their own script and acted out their script on television. Some children were able to use the cameras and, with a little help, some children were able to use the controls in the Control Room. The kids I took were in grades three, four, and five. This was one of the best field trips I have ever taken. I had many purposes for this trip. The children were actively involved in writing as they came up with their own script. There was cooperative learning going on as some students wrote their scripts together. The children chosen to operate cameras got a taste of boss-employee relationship since they had to listen to the director give them directions over the headphones.

As long as you can justify the educational reason for the trip, it is usually accepted.

QUESTION:
How soon can I tell the kids and parents about a field trip?

ANSWER:
Check out the policy for your school from your administrator. Don't tell kids about a field trip without knowing the policy. It could be embarrassing to take back a promised field trip.

QUESTION:
You mean field trips are not always approved?

ANSWER:
Sure, there could be bus problems or insurance risks . Before telling your children, get approval for the trip.

QUESTION:
Do the children pay for the field trip?

ANSWER:
Each school handles this differently. Some schools allow one field trip, some allow two per year. Some pay for the kids, some don't pay for the kids. Ask how it is managed in your particular district.

QUESTION:
I have 26 kids. I'm afraid to be responsible for all of them. What do I do?

ANSWER:
Most districts won't let you go alone. There is usually a student to parent ratio. You need to get parent volunteers.

QUESTION:
How do I get parents to volunteer?

ANSWER:
You will need a permission slip from each child signed by a parent indicating a child has permission to go on the trip. In your letter, you can ask for parent volunteers. Your slip could look like this:

Sample Field Trip Permission Slip

My child has my permission to go on the field trip to _____ on April

10, 200___. I understand it is a full day trip. Therefore, my child will be

responsible for his/her own lunch. I understand my child will be going by bus

and the bus is leaving the school parking lot at 10:00 AM. The bus will return

in time for normal dismissal.

Student Name _____

Parent Signature _____

Emergency Phone Number _____

_____ I am interested in volunteering for this trip.

_____ I am not able to volunteer for this trip.

****This permission slip must be turned in by April 2, 200___.

QUESTION:
Will all the children return their permission slips?

ANSWER:
No, there will be children who forget no matter how many reminders you give them. At this point, you could tell the child, s/he will not be going on the trip. You could ask

another teacher to watch this child for the day. You may want to telephone home and explain to the parent that you need the field trip permission slip. All children who attend a field trip *must have* parental permission.

QUESTION:
Do I need parental permission to visit another school in the same district?

ANSWER:
If you are leaving the building, it is a field trip. If this is the policy in your district, a field trip permission slip is necessary.

QUESTION:
I have students who are on medication during the day. How do I handle this?

ANSWER:
Talk to your school nurse. I know when I have taken children on field trips who are on medication I have had to give meds. It is rare for a teacher to give meds, but this is an exception to the rule.

QUESTION:
Besides getting written permission from parents, is there anything else I need to do?

ANSWER:
Yes, I would contact your bus service two or three days before your field trip. I would then contact them again the day of the field trip. Many children will be disappointed when there is a slip-up on the transportation.

QUESTION:
Once I get parent volunteers, should I put a child with his own parent?

ANSWER:
It depends on the child. Some children behave with you, but not with their parent. You usually don't know this until it's too late. I generally try *not* to put parents with their own child. If a child gives me a hard time in class, then I *do* put that child with his own parent.

QUESTION:
What is my responsibility if I have parents acting as chaperones?

ANSWER:
I try to make it a rule not to have responsibility for any one group. The reason for this is that I am responsible for *all* of the children. It is my job to take care of the sick child, the hurt child, the lost child, etc. You will be busy.

QUESTION:
How do I keep them quiet on the bus ride to our destination?

ANSWER:
It's almost impossible to keep the noise level down. However, before leaving, establish a procedure so they know when you want their attention. For example, I put two to three kids in a seat. They are not allowed to move once seating arrangements have been made. When I want their attention, I stand up. If the bus is moving, and I'm standing, they know there's a problem. They have been told beforehand to look at me and listen for further directions.

QUESTION:
What if they don't quiet down?

ANSWER:

Before you leave on the trip, talk about consequences for inappropriate behavior. Perhaps a child will be isolated and not allowed to have lunch with other children. Perhaps a child will be removed from a bus seat and asked to sit alone. Whatever you do, the rest will calm down. Usually, you only have to make an example out of one child before the rest get the message.

QUESTION:

The parent chaperones are not sitting with their group on the bus. How do I get them back together again?

ANSWER:

This is something you have to pre-plan. Before boarding the bus, explain to the chaperones and kids that once you have reached your destination that all chaperones will get off the bus first. They are to stand in a line and the children will go to them. They are to stay with the chaperone until *you* have counted heads to make sure everyone is accounted for. Before boarding the bus for the ride home, do the same thing. Have the parents stand by the bus. *You* count heads again and make sure everyone is accounted for.

QUESTION:

After the field trip is over, one mom asked me if she could take her son and his friend home. Is that okay to do?

ANSWER:

No, you are not allowed to have a child go home with another student unless there is a note from the parent saying it is permissible. *You* are still responsible for all of the children.

QUESTION:

Some of the parents are going to follow the bus to the field trip. One of the parent's asked if her child could be a passenger in her own car. Is that okay?

ANSWER:

This parent would have to get permission from the principal to drive her own child in the car. The reason for this is that once the child is in school, that child is your legal responsibility . If anything happened while the mom was driving the car, it could be a potential problem.

QUESTION:

How do I keep track of all of the children? If I count heads and come up one short, then what?

ANSWER:

Before you leave on a field trip, make yourself a master list of all the children and the parent chaperone responsible for a group of children. In addition, give each parent chaperone a list of the children s/he is responsible for. Don't overload parents with too many children, three to four children per parent is a good number. If you come up short one child, don't panic. Leave the rest of the children on the bus and retrace your steps. It's always a good idea to go on a field trip with another teacher. If you lose a child, the other teacher can supervise the rest of the children on the bus. Usually, the missing child is in the bathroom or getting a drink. I have been on many field trips and haven't lost a child yet.

QUESTION:

What if the parent lets the kids run off? What do I do?

ANSWER:
You make yourself a mental note *not* to have that parent come again. But in the meantime, stick close by to this particular group of children. That's why you never have a group you are responsible for, since you are responsible for all students.

QUESTION:
Once we return from the field trip, what activities can we do as a group?

ANSWER:
It is always nice to have the children write thank you notes to the parent chaperone. This is a good writing assignment and a good occasion to teach children manners.

QUESTION:
What other follow-up activities can I do?

ANSWER:
Let's say you went to a science museum to learn about constellations. You could put your children in groups and have them write out facts they learned from the guide at the museum. They could decorate a large sheet of paper with constellations and write some facts about the stars.

QUESTION:
Field trips sound stressful. Are they?

ANSWER:
Yes, it's like putting in two days of work. But they are also very rewarding experiences.

Computers

If you are fortunate enough to have a computer in your room, but aren't sure how to use it, find a colleague who uses the computer for educational purposes. Back in the 80's, I was given a computer for my room. I didn't know how to turn it on. I taught myself. You can teach yourself too. It's almost impossible to break the computer. The only caution I have is don't hook it up on your own. I burnt a printer card when I reversed a cord. It was my first day on the job as a "Computer Specialist". Fortunately, they kept me. I stayed on and taught teachers, parents, students, and administrators the many uses of a computer. To this day, I won't put a computer together unless I have one sitting close by that's up, working and not smoking.

QUESTION:
My school has purchased a lot of CD-ROMS. How do I know which CD-ROM to use?

ANSWER:
Figure out what concept you want reinforced. Is it math, reading, science, etc? Find a CD-ROM that will add to your curriculum. Find a half hour of uninterrupted time and use the CD-ROM program. Check out the "teacher features" of the program. Usually, you can set the level of difficulty for the various academic levels in your room.

QUESTION:
But I don't know how to turn the computer on. How am I going to learn how to set difficulty levels for children on CD-ROM?

ANSWER:
Find a student who can teach you how to turn on the computer and show you how to use the CD-ROM. When your class is at gym, library, music, etc. have this student teach you. If you teach younger children, ask someone who has older students for a knowledgeable and patient person. If you are embarrassed since you can't turn on the computer, don't worry. Hand the CD-ROM to the student and watch how he turns the computer on and inserts the CD-ROM. Make sure you watch how he takes the CD-ROM out and turns off the computer.

QUESTION:
I have 24 students and 2 computers. How do I keep track of when everyone uses the computer?

ANSWER:
Put up a chart. List student names and days of the week. Teach the children to put a check mark every time they use the computer.

Sample Computer Usage Chart

Student Name	Mon.	Tues.	Wed.	Thurs.	Fri.
Week of March 1					
Mary A.					
Joe B.					
Frank C.					

QUESTION:
Won't children "forget" to check their name on the graph so they can get more computer time?

ANSWER:
Yes, they will forget. This is a "teachable moment". Talk about honesty and trust. Together with the students, develop consequences which will be taken when children "forget" to indicate they've been on the computer. I can assure you someone will "forget" to be honest. At that time, you must enforce whatever consequence you jointly decided upon. Your children will become less forgetful.

QUESTION:
Should I let my students write stories using the word processor?

ANSWER:
I allow my kids to use the word processor because I can immediately point out and correct student errors that have been made. Some word processing programs have a drawing component. Kids love to draw a picture that goes along with what they have written.

QUESTION:
Do younger students know how to type?

ANSWER:
No, I wish they did. With computer usage continually increasing, I wish school boards would think about offering keyboarding classes for elementary students.

QUESTION:
What about Internet usage? Any policies regarding the internet?

ANSWER:
Because of the non-educational material on the Internet, I think it is important to have policies regulating the use of the Internet. For example, in one school, children are not allowed on the Internet unless they have a signed permission slip from a parent. In addition, certain "safe sites" have been placed on the computer so children can access them quickly.

There are controls you can put on the computer so children cannot go to places you wouldn't want them to access.

QUESTION:
What is a search engine?

ANSWER:
Imagine you're taking a drive on an old country road. There are roads that branch off from the main road. The car you're driving is the "search engine." The side roads are the roads you can take to reach the World Wide Web which has all sorts of information. The abbreviation for the World Wide Web is "www".

QUESTION:
Any examples of search engines?

ANSWER:
Yes, I can give you a few addresses. Keep in mind there are many, many more.
> http://www.metacrawler.com
> http://www.excite.com
> http://www.yahoo.com

QUESTION:
What happens if I type in the wrong address and I miss a period or a colon?

ANSWER:
When this happens you will get an error message. The message will say "incorrect URL address". URL stands for **U**niversal **R**esource **L**ocator. It just means what you typed in was inaccurate. Just retype the address exactly as I've typed it. Don't add any periods or spaces.

QUESTION:
Any other examples of sites that would be of interest to a teacher?

ANSWER:
There are numerous sites. I'll list them according to subject matter. Keep in mind I'm only scratching the surface. As of this publication, all sites are up and working. Keep in mind that since this is the Internet, locations frequently change. You may get a message that says "URL not found". It could be one of two reasons. One, you typed in the address incorrectly, or two, the URL is no longer in existence.

Here are the sites:

General Educational Sites
Lessons This site has practical lesson plans for preschool teachers to undergraduate. The site address is: http://faldo.atmos.uiuc.edu/CLA

Library in the Sky This sites will take you to other sites. It is organized by subject. The site is address is:www.nwrel.org/sky/teacher.html

BlueWeb'n This is a database of Internet learning sites categorized by subject area and audience. The site address is: http://www.kn.pacbell.com/wired/bluewebn

Language Arts
CyberGuides This site has step by step guides for teaching core literature works. They're arranged by grade level. The site address is: http://www.sdcoe.k12.ca.us/score/cyk3.html

Outta Ray's Head Writing Lessons This site covers all aspects of writing. The site address is: http://www3.sympatico.ca/ray.saitz/writing.htm

Science

Science Adventure This site is a database of museums, zoos, aquariums, planetariums across the United States. The site is http://www.scienceadventures.org/

Math

Math Online This site is for grades K–12 and has math lesson plans. The site address is: http://www.kqed.org/cell/math/mathmenu.html

Teacher2Teacher This site is for teachers who need help with a math problem and for students who need assistance. The site address is: http://forum.swarth more.edu/t2t/

Social Studies

History/Social Studies for K–12 Teachers This site has access to lesson plans. The site address is: http://www.execpc.com/~dboals/

QUESTION:
Any other useful sites?

ANSWER:
The Internet School Library Media Center can be accessed by typing: http://www. Falcon.jmu.edu/~ramseyil/

QUESTION:
How do I find safe places for children?

ANSWER:
I'll list a few. Once you have some sites, they usually lead you to other places. These sites include:

> http://www.yaholligans.com

> http://www.ajkids.com

> http://www.night.net

Keep in mind, this is just a few. There are many, many more.

QUESTION:
Is there a site that reviews childrens' software?

ANSWER:
Yes, you could try: http://www.microweb.com/pepsite/Revue/allstar.html

QUESTION:
What about questions I may have regarding state educational guidelines?

ANSWER:
http://www.ed.gov is a good site and will lead you to other sites.

QUESTION:
Are there any courses offered which would teach me how to use the internet?

ANSWER:
http://www.ala.org/ICONN not only teaches you the Internet, but offers a wide variety of additional course descriptions you may want to investigate.

QUESTION:
Are all the sites easy to use?

ANSWER:
Once you get more comfortable using the world wide web, you will take your own shortcuts.

 **Family Suggestions**

Many times parents want to help their children but don't know what to do. This chapter will look at some practical suggestions that you can offer to parents.

QUESTION:
I have a student in kindergarten who doesn't learn as quickly as the rest of the children. He still can't identify the letters of the alphabet. His parents are willing to help him , but I know this child will not sit for any paper and pencil activities. Any suggestions?

ANSWER:
As this child's teacher, you need to identify which letters this child knows and which letters this child doesn't know. All you have to do for a quick assessment is use flash cards with the names of the letters. Ask this student to tell you their names. Don't ask for sounds or words that begin with the letter. Just the name of the letter. Once you have isolated the letters he doesn't know, you will be able to move forward.

One suggestion is to buy an inexpensive book ring from a department store. Get index cards and punch holes in these cards. Put the names of the letters the child **does** know on the ring. It may be only three letters, but it's a start. Next, invite the parents in to show them the letter ring you have for their child. Ask the parents to add a letter from the list you've made of the letters the child doesn't know. Every time the child is able to identify the letter, he will get a star. After getting five stars, encourage the parents to add another letter that the child is unfamiliar with. You must encourage the parents to move very slowly with this child. This child already has tasted defeat.

In addition to calling out the letters, parents may want to use another approach. Some students love to get their hands into everything. Ask the parents to get a can of shaving cream. Spread shaving cream on a TV tray table and have the child form the letters he already knows and identify them by name. Slowly introduce letters he is not familiar with. Introducing new letters must be done gradually, or the student will become frustrated. Another strategy is to have the student find letters in an advertisement. For example, when the Sunday paper comes with all of the ads, have this child look for words that have the letter "B" in them, if that is the letter he knows or is working on. Have the child sort words according to where the letter "B" is located in the word. For example:

ball	ta**b**le	cri**b**
bat	a**b**acus	cra**b**

I know the child will not be able to read these words. But the purpose is just to show the child that letters make up words. Eventually curiosity will take over and the child may ask his parents what the words are. This is what is called a "teachable " moment. You encourage parents to take it, and run with it.

QUESTION:

What about students who know their letter names, but don't understand that those letters make up words? How do I have parents help their child with this?

ANSWER:

Have parents use a very simple rhyming book with these children. For example, let's try Jack and Jill.

> Jack and Jill
>
> Went up the hill
>
> To fetch a pail of water

Have the parents ask their child how many *words* are in the first line. I have done this in a kindergarten classroom and I have gotten some interesting answers. Some children will tell me 3 words and I'm ready to celebrate until I tell them to count them for me. This is what they do this:

J a c k   a n d   J i l l

1 2 3

Children need to be taught that the space between the letters means that the word has ended and a new word has begun. You see it as an adult, but a child needs to be taught this concept. Have parents count out the words with their children. Once they are finished counting, have them read the nursery rhyme and point to the individual word as it is being read. Eventually, the child will "read" the rhyme to the parent. Yes, I know it has been memorized, but many words in our language need to be memorized because they make no phonetic sense. Look at the word "the", you can't sound it out.

QUESTION:

Any suggestions on how to teach a child reading skills outside of the classroom?

ANSWER:

Yes, when my son was younger he would want everything in sight at the grocery store. I would bring coupons with me for certain kid food such as cookies, ice cream, etc. He had to match the coupon with the cookie brand and then I would buy it. Now sometimes he would bring Keebler chocolate chip cookies and the coupon was for Nabisco chocolate chip cookies. I didn't buy the cookies until he had done the matching correctly. Could he read the two words? No, but he began to make some sense out of the written language since he had a purpose for knowing our language. My rule was: No match, no cookies. I did the same thing when we were in the cereal aisle. He had to match my coupon with the cereal brand. Encourage parents to place the child somewhere near the item or it can be very frustrating.

QUESTION:

Any other grocery shop strategies?

ANSWER:

Yes, when an item has run out of your household, have the child cut the name of the item out from the box and put it in an envelope. When it's time to shop, this envelope goes with you and the child once again matches the item from his envelope to the grocery store product. These are very simple, inexpensive things all parents can do.

QUESTION:
What about older children who are struggling with reading?

ANSWER:
Let's suppose you have a child in fifth grade who is reading on a third grade level. Parents can take their child to the library and have the child select a book on whatever subject the child is interested in. Let's suppose it's soccer. What if the child selects a book that is too difficult? The parent can get the difficult book, as well as another book on soccer that the child will have less difficulty reading. If the child makes a scene about the parent's suggestion, take the book anyway. Now what do you do with it? With the harder book, have the parents read along with the child. This method is called shared reading. The parent is sharing the reading with the child. You actually read the words together. When a child is having difficulty with a word, the parent nonchalantly supplies the word and keeps reading. Don't have the child sound it out, just keep reading.

With the easier book that the parent selected, have the parent casually look through it with the child. The child will probably want to read this book and be very happy that s/he can read it alone.

QUESTION:
I have a student who loves to do crafts, but has a difficult time reading. Any ideas for this parent?

ANSWER:
Yes. Since this parent is willing to buy crafts for this child, invite the parents to take the next step. Have them go to the library and find books on this particular craft. Have the parents try to get a book that is on the child's reading level if at all possible. If they can't find that book, ask the parents to sit and read with the child. The child needs to see the connection between what they enjoy and what they can learn from reading a book on that subject. Interest is a powerful motivator.

QUESTION:
Parents don't seem to understand that taking kids places is valuable. How do I convince them of the importance of taking their children to museums, libraries, etc. instead of just the video store?

ANSWER:
Usually all schools have an open house during the first month of school. At this time, you can explain to parents how the experiences they provide for their children help shape them. When you discuss things at school, it's important for their child to have some background knowledge on the subject. For example, visiting a zoo helps the child know about different animals and their habitats. Visiting a science museum helps them understand more about the unit on electricity or communication, or whatever content area you will be studying. Sometimes parents just don't *know* that this type of "parental field trip" helps their child. You also might want to encourage them to get a library card from their local library. I have had many parents tell me they didn't know they could borrow books for free. They thought they had to pay for the service. Most parents are caring people who just don't know what is available to them. It's through your efforts they will learn about the many services accessible to them.

QUESTION:
I have children who are of a different faith than most children. They do not celebrate the traditional holidays such as Thanksgiving, Easter and Christmas. What do I do when these holidays come around?

ANSWER:

Different schools have different policies. For example, I know of a school that forbids celebration of any holidays. In doing so, there is no conflict, because holidays are not observed. In another school, the holidays are celebrated, but those children who have a different faith leave and spend time at the office or parents pick them up and take them home. It is important to find out what the policy is in your particular school. Usually a fellow teacher will know how these festivities are handled.

QUESTION:

I know of a family who would benefit from family counseling? How do I handle this?

ANSWER:

You need to be clear in your own mind the purpose for your recommendation. If you have a school counselor, you may want to suggest to the parent that s/he talk to the school counselor. The counselor will be familiar with outside agencies for additional assistance.

If you don't have a counselor, you will have to help this person locate the needed help. Try not to recommend a specific counselor in case there is a personality conflict.

How To Keep

Your Stress Down

 **Classroom Management**

You must have a clearly defined management system in place. Without it, learning will not occur. You will have chaos. I know, because my first few weeks of my first year were chaotic. I thought everyone would come in ready, willing, and able to learn. I was wrong! They came in ready, willing, and able to see what they could get away with! Read some of the classroom tips below.

QUESTION:
It's September and I want to get the school year off on the right foot. How do I introduce the rules of the room?

ANSWER:
An effective tool I've used is to have the children involved in making the rules. Explain to them that you will be living together for ten months so there must be rules that everyone can live with. Talk about some of the things that you may need rules for. Illicit from the children what rules they think are important. For example:

Sample Class Rules	
BEHAVIOR	CONSEQUENCES
1. When someone is talking, all hands should be down, and pay attention to what the person is saying.	1. One check 2. Two checks 3. Name on board 4. Lose free time.
2. When the bell rings, everyone must be in their seats.	

You will make approximately five rules for the class to live by. Any more than that causes another set of problems. They forget what they are supposed to do. Students as young as kindergarten and as old as twelfth grade can make rules. Then, together, set up consequences for children who do not follow the rules.

QUESTION:
With the consequences that you set , some children may not care if their name is on the board. Then what?

ANSWER:
You are absolutely right! Some children need a heavier consequence. You can always have them write a note home about their inappropriate behavior that needs to be signed by a parent. This is very effective with most children. Always photo copy this paper because the paper tends to get lost or forgotten. The paper could look like the one below.

Sample Student Note to Parent

My teacher asked me to _____

_____

Instead I _____

Parent Signatue _____

Date _____

QUESTION:
How do I keep track of everyone's papers? I am forever correcting papers and can't remember who gave me what paper. Is there a simple way to keep track?

ANSWER:
I have found that asking children to put their name and then a number on the paper is effective. For example, once you are sure of your enrollment (give it about a week), alphabetize everyone and number each child. For example Joe Andrew is #1, and Mary Brown is #2. When the children hand in their papers, they are to put the papers in numerical order. You can tell at a quick glance who forgot to hand in a paper. On the board, have a separate spot for "Late Papers". Write the student's name or number on the board. The only person who can erase the name is the teacher. I didn't like giving kids numbers because I felt you get enough of that when you go to college. However, it is the only way I know of to do a quick check on class work.

QUESTION:
As soon as the children get off the bus they are handing me papers that are from their parent or homework assignments. Is there an easier way to handle all the paperwork?

ANSWER:
Have a box on your desk that is labeled "Papers From Home". You may want two separate boxes: one for parent notes and one for late assignments. Direct the children to put the notes in the box. When you get a free minute, you can look at them.

QUESTION:
We have to do lunch count and attendance every day. How can I make the job easier?

ANSWER:
It always impresses me when I see children doing that very job. Children as young as first grade have taken care of lunch count and attendance. They need to be taught , but it appears to be well worth the apprenticeship. Keep it simple and kids can do anything. How do you teach the kids to take attendance? Model for them what they need to do.

QUESTION:
Should I put the kids in rows or pairs? Which way is best?

ANSWER:
This depends on your own preference and what you can live with. Both ways have advantages and disadvantages. In rows, kids are usually better disciplined because there isn't anyone to get in trouble with. However, in pairs, it is easier to do cooperative learning. As long as you have a discipline code in place, either way will work.

You could start out with rows and slowly move those *deserving* students into pairs. Or, you could start out with pairs and slowly move those *undeserving* students out of pairs. I've done it both ways.

QUESTION:
I have a student no one likes. They don't want to sit next to her or work with her. This girl is a bit of a problem. She causes trouble all the time. What can I do to help her and help the rest of the class?

ANSWER:
I have talked to my whole class when the "disruptive" child is not around. At times I have asked another teacher to keep this child busy. I center the discussion on how we want to be treated. We have discussed ways to make the child feel comfortable. When the disruptive child is back, I praise those children that have been kind to her/him.

In addition, I pull the "disruptive child" away from the group and talk to this person alone. It may be during a gym period for the rest of the class. I explain how the kids want to be her/his friend. This *usually* works, but sometimes it doesn't.

There are some children who have such problems that they will fight you all the way. I know that I can go to sleep at night knowing that I did try and that my students tried their best also. I think that's the most you could hope for. I recently had a student who would not accept anyone's friendship. I know my kids tried. From a distance, I observed everyone's behavior. I went home upset but, until the "disruptive" child wants to give it a go, you will have a hard time. Someone once told me the results of my efforts may not be shown to me. I keep this thought with me when I feel I have failed a child.

QUESTION:
I want to ask questions orally after a science unit. What's the best way to insure that all students are listening?

ANSWER:
I saw an interesting technique in a classroom. The teacher had each child's name on a popsicle stick (art stick). The popsicle sticks were then placed in a cup. The teacher would ask a question and pull a popsicle stick out of the can. This child had to answer the question. This kept everyone on his/her toes since a child didn't know when his name would be called. Once they were called on, the popsicle stick went right back in the cup. In doing so, children weren't off the hook. They still had to listen. The teacher could pull the same stick again. I thought it was a great idea.

QUESTION:
We have children who are bused in and out of school. How do I handle who is on what bus, especially in September?

ANSWER:
This is *the* most frustrating part of the day. I suggest that, before the buses come, do a head check. Make sure the bus they think they are going home on is the bus you think they are going on. Then, at the end of the day, line the students up according to the

number of bus they are on. For example, Bus 1, then Bus 2 or Bus A, Bus B, etc. If you have younger children, (kindergarten , first grade) try to get older children to act as helpers. The older children will have the names of the younger children who they are responsible for. For example, if Mary in grade 5 takes Bus 1 home, she will take with her all the younger children that go home on Bus 1. This is usually three to four kids. Then Bill in grade 5 will take Bus 2 children, and so forth.

The first day is total confusion. The second day is less confusing. By the end of the week, everyone is happy. Just check *everything* before the buses arrive. By the way, for the first week of school, busses are usually late. Just expect it.

QUESTION:
My kindergarten students are bused in to school and out of school? How do I keep this all straight?

ANSWER:
You don't have to worry about the bus they come to school on. You only need to be concerned about the bus they leave on. Here's a plan to teach the younger children, let's say kindergarten, which bus to board. *Before* it is time to leave, have a practice run. Give each child who rides Bus 1, a red apple; Bus 2 a green apple; etc. Then you hold up a large red apple, then green apple. When the children see you hold up the red apple, it is time for them to line up. When you hold up the green apple, those children line up. Now, getting them to the bus in one piece is another story. If you are lucky enough to have older children, enlist their help. Give them a red apple, green apple, etc. too. They will take those children to that bus. If you don't have an older student, you'll have to do this yourself—just tell the kids to stick with you. They are usually so scared, they won't leave your side. Have the child's name and bus number in writing , so you'll know for sure which bus a child rides. I can promise some students will misplace their apples. It happens all the time.

QUESTION:
Parents come to my room to pick up their children at the end of the day. Should I let them go right to their parents?

ANSWER:
Usually NO!!! The reason is many children have custody restraints. Mom can pick up or Dad can pick up. If Mom can't pick up and she shows up at your door and you don't know Mom doesn't have permission to take her child, you could have a big problem. Tell all parents they must go to the office and have the office personnel call for the child.

Most parents accept this and appreciate it. However, I still remember when I refused a parent, he got very angry. I didn't know *he* was the one who could pick up the child. Instead of thanking me for taking care of his child, he got mad. Expect that too—anger when you are doing the best you know for the child.

QUESTION:
What if a children says he goes on Bus 1, but my note says Bus 2?

ANSWER:
That's why you do the dry run *before* the bus is actually there. You'll find all sorts of mistakes. Do it before the bus comes and you'll have less hassle. If a child is insisting, ask the bus driver which streets s/he travels on. Perhaps for one day, the child can be transported on this bus until the situation is cleared up.

QUESTION:
If I find a bus inconsistency, who do I tell?

ANSWER:
Usually the office personnel handle this problem. If they don't, they will pass it on to the person who does take care of the matter.

QUESTION:
We have outside lockers for the students. How am I supposed to monitor children in the room and out of the room?

ANSWER:
You stand right in the doorway. In doing so, you see what is going on in both places. Or you may want a responsible child to be the "patrol" for the week. They watch the children outside by the lockers. Once the children come in, have something purposeful for them to do. Even if you want them to sit and talk with one other person, that's very purposeful. Just don't give them idle time. Idle time x 26 kids= problems

QUESTION:
How do I maintain discipline when I'm walking in the halls with my children?

ANSWER:
Before you leave your classroom, explain what you expect from your students as they walk in the halls. Where do you expect them to put their hands? Tell them. Can they touch the papers hanging on the walls? If not, tell them. Can they pull the shirt of the child ahead of them? Tell them. Can they give a high-five to the children that are walking in the opposite direction? Tell them. Let them know exactly what you expect from them. Have consequences for children who do not follow your directions.

Also, where you walk is important. Do *not* walk at the front of the line. The children behind you will realize you can't see them and may become mischievous. Walk either at the end of the line, or at the middle of the line. If you walk at the end, have a line leader who you have told to stop at certain spots along the way to your destination. The reason you stop at certain spots is to keep your line together. If you walk at the middle of the line, keep turning back to check the children behind you.

I have also seen teachers who have student monitors. The teacher walks at the end of the line and has a student monitor walking alongside the class to remind children what proper behavior is supposed to look like. When you get to a corner, you stand at the corner until both groups have passed that area. This way you can see both groups at once. If you go around the corner, anything could happen with the children who haven't reached that point.

QUESTION:
Children get off the bus and are allowed to come to the room at 8:30 a.m. I'm always in my room by 8:30 a.m., however, sometimes children get dropped off by parents and they show up at 8:25 a.m. What do I do about this?

ANSWER:
On the first day of school, explain to children where they are to stand when you are *not* in the room. Tell them they are *not* allowed in the room until you are there. The reason for this is liability. You are responsible for the children from 8:30 a.m. until the end of your school day. I ask my students to wait in the hall outside the classroom. Although they have been told this over and over, there are still children who will go looking for me. After receiving the agreed upon consequences, they realize where they must stand.

QUESTION:
Children are always getting out of their seat to sharpen pencils when there is a paper and pencil activity. Any suggestions?

ANSWER:
Some teachers require children to have five sharpened pencils each morning. Why five pencils? By noon, three of those pencils are broken. There will be children who have only one pencil to sharpen. They should sit down to write a note telling their parent they need more pencils. In the meantime, children will share pencils.

QUESTION:
What is wait time?

ANSWER:
After you ask a student a question, allow some time for the child to formulate an answer. This time is called "wait time". Expecting a child to answer immediately will prove to be frustrating not only for the child, but also for you, as the teacher.

QUESTION:
How do I get my children to cooperatively work in groups?

ANSWER:
Cooperation is a "skill" that must be taught to children. There are books on this subject, (see Additional Suggested Readings section at the end of this book.) but I will touch on the answer. Begin your groups with a small number of children. Let's agree upon four children. One child is the teacher, one child is the note taker, and all four children are contributors to the conversation. Let's say the topic is "What other uses can you come up with for a pencil?" All children will give answers. They must be taught all answers are acceptable. The note taker writes down all answers. The teacher of the group keeps the conversation on the topic.

QUESTION:
Who decides the roles of each child?

ANSWER:
You teach the children to do this on their own. How? Model it , use four children as an example and talk the class through it.

QUESTION:
Doesn't everyone want to be the teacher or note taker?

ANSWER:
Yes, so expect disagreements. The children will get better at cooperative learning the more you have them work together in groups. It is worth the initial aggravation.

QUESTION:
What is the most difficult aspect of teaching?

ANSWER:
Classroom management is the most difficult aspect of teaching. You need to cooperatively develop rules and consequences. Once this has been established, follow through. Teaching will be much easier if everyone knows what the expectations are in the classroom.

Discipline and All That Jazz

In order for your classroom to run smoothly, you must have a discipline routine to follow. Without discipline, you will have chaos.

QUESTION:
I am having a hard time maintaining discipline in my class of 25 third graders. They are constantly talking while I'm talking. What do I do?

ANSWER:
You need to talk with your class about what is acceptable and what isn't acceptable. Then, have them come up with rules *with* you. In doing this, there is ownership in the class. Talk about consequences for bad behavior and most important , follow through. It is a good idea to make no more than five rules with the children. Any more rules and they won't remember them. Make sure you have the rules and consequences written for everyone to see. Sometimes you have to make an example out of one child who chooses to break a rule. The rest will then understand that you mean business.

QUESTION:
What are my chances of getting a student who won't listen to me?

ANSWER:
Statistics have been done about the number of children who follow the rules. The numbers are 80% follow rules without any problems, 15% follow rules sporadically, and 5% won't follow your rules. But the 5% usually like company along the way, so they'll encourage other children not to listen to you.

QUESTION:
Is there a way I can set the tone on the first day?

ANSWER:
Yes, tell them they look like the best class you have ever had. Tell them what wonderful things you have heard about them. Don't be fake, ask other teachers what positive things they can tell you about some of the children. You need to build up a trust level. It is so important for them to trust you. You have to mean what you say and say what you mean.

QUESTION:
How do I build up a trust level?

ANSWER:
Catch them being good and tell them how good they are. If someone gets a pencil for

another student who dropped one, reinforce in front of the class what a kind person Joey is for picking up Mary's pencil. Just catch them being good and expect good.

QUESTION:

It seems I spend so much of my day disciplining children that the good kids don't get any attention. How can I change this? Help!

ANSWER:

Compliment the good kids as often as you can. Don't take good behavior for granted. There is that 5 % that is waiting to take the good kids along. Keep reinforcing positive behavior.

QUESTION:

I have a child who is constantly tripping other children. When s/he is confronted, it's always, "I didn't do nothin." What do I do since I usually miss the incident?

ANSWER:

You may want to talk with this child alone and try to get him/her to admit what is going on, especially if you suspect that the other children are telling the truth. This works most of the time. If the child won't admit to it, you need to bring the other children into the conversation and try to tactfully talk things out without accusing anyone. If the child admits to tripping children, then pull him/her aside and talk about consequences of the behavior. If the child doesn't admit to it, watch that child closely, sooner or later s/he'll make a mistake.

QUESTION:

I have a child who is disruptive and is also a child of a very outspoken board member. What do I do?

ANSWER:

You have to treat all children the same way. Do not show favoritism. If the child is misbehaving, talk to this parent as you would any other parent. But first tell your administrator that you are planning on having this conversation with the parent. Remember, administrators can not support you, if they don't know there is a problem.

QUESTION:

I have a child who is very argumentative. His attitude ruins my day. Can you help?

ANSWER:

In order for this child to argue, s/he must have someone to argue with. When you ask Joey to get his social studies book out and he tells you no, remind him of the consequences on the rules chart that was made by the entire class. At this point, he will probably tell you he doesn't care. You repeat what you want him to do for the second time. If he still doesn't do it, give him the consequence for the action. Do *not* argue. Just firmly tell him what he is going to do. You won't feel too good doing this, but it needs to be done. He cannot *win* this, you *must* win. When he is on task, congratulate him for his good behavior. He may shrug his shoulders as if he doesn't care. Don't buy it, he does care. He just isn't used to positive reinforcement. Later on, when things have cooled down, talk to him about what happened earlier. Kids have told me , "I was mad, that's what I do when I'm mad." I reply with, "Okay, but that's what I do when you aren't listening."

QUESTION:

I have a child who is constantly taking things out of other childrens' desks. No amount of warnings have stopped this child. S/he admits it, but what do I do now?

ANSWER:

I have found an effective tool to use. Have the child write down what s/he did wrong on paper. An example of this is in the Classroom Management chapter on page 132.

Take the paper, make a copy of it and tell the child this paper must go home and get signed. The reason you make the copy is that sometimes papers tend to get "lost". Usually, you will get a phone call or a letter from the parent about the shoplifting. Again, tell your administrator because this is a situation that could escalate. If the signed paper does not come back, call the parent at home and leave a message asking the parent to call the school. Do not explain on an answering machine what the phone call is all about. Just a simple, "Hi, I'm so and so's teacher and please call the school. This is not an emergency. The number is 555-5555." If the parent still doesn't call, it's time for administrator intervention. Most parents will call an administrator. However, use the administrator as a last resort.

QUESTION:

Is it possible for one child to upset a whole classroom? I am relieved when one particular child in my class is absent.

ANSWER:

One child can upset an entire room. I know the guilt and relief I feel when that child is absent. However, I try to look for the good in each child. Try to talk to that child alone and figure out why the child is misbehaving. Usually there is a problem at home that needs to be solved. First, call home and talk to the parents. This usually goes a long way. But if that fails, enlist the help of the school counselor. Try to be nice to this child. As hard as it is for you to be in the same room as this child, it is that hard for that child to be good, whatever the reasons are. Someone once told me that I can't save everyone, but you have to treat everyone with respect. That's the best solution I can offer.

QUESTION:

I have a child who is always causing problems. When I mention it to the parents, they make me feel as though it is my fault that their child is misbehaving. Any suggestions?

ANSWER:

I know how it feels to be on the receiving end of that conversation. I have had to tell parents that their child was misbehaving only to be told by the parent , "I don't know, s/he never did that last year." A solution I found that works 99% of the time is to have the child fill out the form found on page 132, Classroom Management chapter.

QUESTION:

If I send that home, won't the parents get mad at me?

ANSWER:

Probably, they will be angry. But your role as teacher is to provide an education for *all* of your students. You may have one parent angry, but you will have 24 other happy parents since you have tried to maintain discipline and educate *all* children.

QUESTION:

Should I let my principal know if I am sending home a note to a parent?

ANSWER:

When an unfavorable note goes home, I would suggest you let your principal know. Your principal might want you to use a different avenue before the note is sent home. Also, your principal has the right to know what goes on in the building. A principal can't support you if they don't know what is going on. That advice was given to me as a first year teacher and I've used that suggestion with every unfavorable note I've sent home.

QUESTION:

I have a student who sets off my class in a negative way. The kids are beginning to resent this child. How do I get this child to be part of our school family?

ANSWER:

First, you need to try and figure out where this child is coming from . Bad behavior is a symptom of something else. As the teacher, try to figure out what the something else is. Perhaps his favorite grandpa died. Perhaps his parents are going through a divorce. It could be something as easy as a change in medication due to a bad cold. It could be any number of things. Once you have determined what the cause is, try to work on solving the problem. Sometimes you can't figure out what the problem is, and those are the kids that are very *hard* to reach. You could try putting that child on a behavior modification program. This will be discussed in more detail at the end of this chapter.

QUESTION:

I have tried isolating a child when the behavior became disruptive, but I always feel bad about it. Any other way to curb this negative behavior?

ANSWER:

Sometimes as teachers we have to do things that we don't want to do. Isolation is an effective tool, especially if the isolation is done to a child who hates to be alone. Put aside your feelings and do what is best for the child in the long run. Remember you have other children who want to learn and one bad apple *can* spoil the apple cart.

QUESTION:

Should I send disruptive kids to the principal's office?

ANSWER:

I use the principal very sparingly for three reasons. One, the principal has a lot to do and you don't want to take too much time out of their busy schedule. Second, it looks as though you can't handle the problem on your own. Third, if you do decide to use the principal, do it infrequently. The kids may think it's not a big deal if you do it all the time. Usually, I use the principal once a year. I go in and say, "I need help." I then tell her what I have done so far and how it has worked, or not worked.

QUESTION:

What is behavior modification?

ANSWER:

There have been books written on this topic. I'll try and explain it in a few sentences. You may have a student whose behavior you want to modify or change. For example, you may have a student who consistently says nasty things to other children. You have called home, talked to your principal, talked to the child and still the inappropriate behavior continues. It is time to try behavior modification. Keep in mind, I'm trying to simplify this. You would talk to this child and find out something this child finds important and worth working toward. For example, something as simple as using the computer for 10 minutes uninterrupted is important to children. You tell the child, s/he must not be nasty to another child for one day and the reward will be given. Then, after you have met with success, change the limit to two days in a row, then three days in a row. Soon, hopefully, the inappropriate behavior will be gone.

QUESTION:

You make it sound so simple, does it work?

ANSWER:
With some kids, it does work. With other kids, it doesn't . You have to remember that some children come to school with many problems and will fight all authority figures.

QUESTION:
What do I do if behavior modification doesn't work?

ANSWER:
Go to your administrator and ask for advice on how to handle this child. If your administrator gives you no support, document it. It is important to document this because the child may hurt someone and at least you will have documentation that you did ask for help, but none was given.

QUESTION:
Won't the rest of the children resent the child who gets a reward for being good?

ANSWER:
Usually the rest of the class is so relieved that the "disruptive" child is finally listening, they don't make a fuss about it. But, sometimes there is a problem. You just have to explain that we all learn differently and this is the way you need to teach "Joey." Try to give some incentive to the rest of the class while "Joey" is getting his positive reward.

QUESTION:
What is the hardest part about teaching children?

ANSWER:
For me, teaching children is easy once you have your discipline policy in place. Take your time discussing discipline and consequences for inappropriate behavior. If you follow through on consequences, teaching becomes very easy.

 **Time Management**

When you realize all that has to be completed by the end of the year, it seems overwhelming. When I begin the school year with my kids, I see what they know and I know where they have to be, I feel as if I will never get them there. Every year, I feel the same way. But at the end of the year, it all comes together. We get to where we are going. How do I do it? Read on.

QUESTION:
How am I to get through all of the required material in a 6 1/2 hour day? It seems impossible.

ANSWER:
It does seem impossible, but pacing is what you need to do. For instance, in an elementary building you have all subjects to cover. The most important academic subjects are reading and math. It makes sense to teach these subjects in the morning when most children are fresh and ready to go. Manage your time so that your children are working purposefully during the early part of the day. Teach reading and math during these precious morning hours.

QUESTION:
What about science, social studies, language arts, and writing? How am I supposed to fit them in?

ANSWER:
You can teach social studies and science through your reading. It may be tricky, but it can be done. Find books that are on grade level or below grade level and use them for two purposes—to teach reading and to teach social studies. Language arts and writing are taught along with reading. There is more on this in the chapter titled Reading on page 98.

QUESTION:
I have kids who can't read the social studies text alone. How am I supposed to teach reading using a text they can't read?

ANSWER:
You don't use that text. You find a book that has the same subject matter, but at a lower level. Or you may want to pair your children and have some students reading to other students.

QUESTION:
What if I don't accomplish everything I wrote down in my planbook?

ANSWER:
Don't worry, just rewrite that portion for the next week.

QUESTION:
I feel as though I'm always correcting papers. The kids look at the grade on the paper and then throw the paper out. I feel like it's a waste of my time. Is it?

ANSWER:
It is a waste of your time. There is another way to handle this. You could have the children correct their own papers. Set aside a desk with a green pen and answer sheet. Children will know immediately what they have done wrong. They can get help from you or from another student. Another way to correct papers is to correct them together and have children fix their mistakes. There are some papers you will need to correct on your own. But children can do a lot, if you allow them. Remember not all papers need to be put in your grade book. Children are learning and shouldn't be penalized for that learning. They are going to make mistakes.

QUESTION:
I have parent volunteers. Can I have them correct my papers?

ANSWER:
I don't think that is a good idea. It is best if *you* know how a student is doing, and not a parent. Sometimes parents talk with one another and you don't want a child's grades being discussed.

 **Safety**

As a teacher, you are responsible for the safety of all your children. Below are some suggestions of ways you can keep everyone as safe as possible.

QUESTION:
I wanted to copy some papers at the office. My classroom is right next to the office. Is it okay to leave the room for one minute? I have wonderful students who will behave.

ANSWER:
It isn't a question of having behaved students. The problem is accidents happen. If you were to leave your room and leave the children unattended and something happened, you would be liable. The rule is *never* leave children unattended. *Never*!

QUESTION:
What if I have to go to the bathroom? Can I leave them alone while I run to the bathroom?

ANSWER:
No, you can't leave children alone. You must get another adult to watch the children. It can not be a parent. It must be a teacher. If you leave, and something happens, once again you are responsible.

QUESTION:
I teach primary grade children and I want to buy a rug to sit on during story hour. Is that okay?

ANSWER:
Schools purchase a certain type of rug that meets regulations. If you were to buy a rug and it didn't have the specifications needed, you would be wasting your money since you would be asked to take the rug back home.

QUESTION:
What about pillows? Can I buy pillows to lay on?

ANSWER:
No, pillows also have to meet fire code rules. In addition, some children may be allergic to some of the substances pillows are made of. Also, lice can be carried on pillows.

QUESTION:
What can I buy? How about a bookshelf for all my books?

ANSWER:
If the bookshelf is *not* taller than the child, it can be left free standing. If it *is* taller than the child, it needs to be bolted into the wall. If it is bolted into the wall and you are asked to leave that room at the end of the year, it is likely your bookshelf will stay.

QUESTION:
I bought a stuffed animal for the children to take home and read to every night. I want to give each child an opportunity to take the stuffed animal home. Is that okay?

ANSWER:
No, stuffed animals going from home to home are going to get dirty. The stuffed toy could also pick up lice and lice would travel from home to home. You don't need to keep your classroom as sterile as a hospital, but you do need to be aware of cleanliness for the sake of all.

QUESTION:
What about pets in school? I have a little girl who wants to bring her fish in.

ANSWER:
Fish are okay, dogs and cats are not okay. If the animal could possibly hurt someone, it can't come into a school building. If the animal could carry something that a child could be allergic to, it can not come into the building. Fish are about the only thing I know of that are safe.

QUESTION:
What about students with food allergies? What do I do at birthday time?

ANSWER:
A parent will usually tell you if their child is allergic to a particular food. Ask this parent to bring in a box of treats for her child only. When it is birthday time, offer this child a treat from the box her parent brought in. *Safety* of the child has to always be on your mind.

QUESTION:
Can I pass out snacks as a treat?

ANSWER:
You can, but you are running the risk of a child being allergic to something you bring in. Also, I never let the kids eat hard candy in my room. When my niece was young, she almost choked on a piece of hard candy. From that day on, I have never allowed hard candy in my room.

QUESTION:
Why can't I hang papers and decorations on my wooden door?

ANSWER:
Because of the fire code, if there was a fire, the paper would burn quickly on the door. Since the paper would burn, the door would ignite swiftly. Keep all papers off your door.

QUESTION:
Can I put a decoration on the window in the door?

ANSWER:
That's not a good idea. Another adult should always be able to see in your room so that you are never suspected of child abuse. It is also a good idea to teach with your door open for the same reason.

QUESTION:

My room gets very hot. Why isn't there a screen on the fire escape window? I want the fresh air, but not the bees.

ANSWER:

If there was ever a fire, children might have to use the fire escape window. Not only should there be no screen, but you also need to keep the shelf by the fire escape window clear at all times. That means no books, no papers, nothing, on the shelf by that window.

QUESTION:

My room gets very hot during the summer months. Can I bring a fan in for comfort?

ANSWER:

No, children can easily poke their fingers through the slots. Even if it looks like it's impossible to poke anything through, a child may be able to figure out a way. This would be a problem.

QUESTION:

I have a cute reading lamp that I want to put in my reading center. Is that okay?

ANSWER:

I'm sorry to say, it's not okay. Lamps are electrical appliances and need to meet certain regulations. Before you bring in anything from home, check with your administrator.

Preparation and Lunch Period

As a teacher you are entitled to a preparation period (prep period) during the school day. Each school system allows a different amount of time. The amount of time given will be stipulated in your contract.

QUESTION:
What is a preparation period?

ANSWER:
A preparation period is a period of time allowed per day for you to prepare for your students. Your students will be taught by the library, music, art or physical education teacher. This time is called your prep period.

QUESTION:
How much time am I able to have?

ANSWER:
That depends on your district and what has been negotiated with your union. Ask a colleague what your contract has written about prep periods.

QUESTION:
What do I do during this period?

ANSWER:
Whatever you want to do—it is *your* time. By the time you take the children to their special, you will want to run to the bathroom and maybe get a can of pop. You won't have a lot of time left, but it gives you a necessary breather.

QUESTION:
Can administrators ask to see mé during prep time?

ANSWER:
Yes, and you can make an appointment to see them too.

QUESTION:
What about lunch? Do I eat with the kids?

ANSWER:
You take the children to lunch and someone is there to monitor them. You have your lunch in a separate room. When the lunch period is over, you pick up your children. Each district has lunch procedures. Ask a colleague about the procedure.

QUESTION:

What if a student forgets his lunch? Do I have to buy lunch for that student?

ANSWER:

No, schools usually have a policy to give children a lunch note. They buy lunch and take the note home to have their parents reimburse the school. Find out what your school policy is.

QUESTION:

Are kids allowed to share their food at lunch?

ANSWER:

Most schools have a policy of not sharing, but kids often share food despite this policy.

Organizational Skills

In order to make teaching easier, you must be organized. You need to be able to put your hands on teaching materials quickly. By June, my desk is disorganized. I usually end up saying, "Oh that's where that is." Here are a few tips to keep yourself together.

QUESTION:
Teachers have told me to keep a folder on each child. Why?

ANSWER:
During parent conferences, you may want to show a parent how you came up with a specific grade. You do *not* need to keep all of their papers, but if you notice a child is having difficulty in math and consistently gets below grade, you may want to keep math papers to explain to the parent how you arrived at the grade. Also, any paper that a parent has signed should be kept because a parent may say I didn't know he was doing poorly. By keeping the paper in the folder, you can say, "You signed the paper." It makes life easier for you.

QUESTION:
How do I organize the child's folder?

ANSWER:
Keep file folders on each child. Print the child's last name , first name on the folder in pencil. Use pencil so that you can reuse the folder for the next year. Keep a pile of papers that need to be filed and whenever you have a minute, file them. Or, if you are lucky enough to have a teacher's aide, ask the aide to file papers when there is a spare minute.

QUESTION:
How do I keep track of when a paper is done? The kids don't always put the date on.

ANSWER:
I purchased a date stamper at the grocery store. The kids love to use it. All of my students' papers are stamped with the date. Their fingers and arms usually get stamped too. That's another one of those rules you make—only the paper, not your body!

QUESTION:
I have received many catalogues from publishers. How do I file them?

ANSWER:
I file them alphabetically. If I know I won't use that publisher, I ask my colleagues if they are interested.

QUESTION:
Should I keep the absence notes the kids give me?

ANSWER:
Check out your school policy. In my building they are usually collected once a month and filed.

QUESTION:
How should I organize my room?

ANSWER:
Categorize your room. I have many many childrens' books. I categorize the books by grade level and put them on the shelf that way. One teacher bought colored sticky dots and put dots in her books according to genre. For example, animal books had a blue dot, fairy tales had a green dot, etc. When children put a book away they matched the book with the colored dot found on the shelf. I also have many games. I place them on my shelf and take a few out at a time for the kids to use. I put all of my school supplies (pencils, paper, staples, paper clips, etc.) on a shelf by itself. Look over your room and put similar things together. You will save yourself a lot of time looking for something when you need it.

QUESTION:
What about all the bulletin boards I have to create? Where do I put them?

ANSWER:
You could buy large boxes and put bulletin boards in them according to month. The September box might have welcome back material. The October box may have Halloween and Fall material. By keeping everything organized, all you have to do is locate the box.

QUESTION:
How do I get the children to bring home notes to their parents?

ANSWER:
Some kids are magicians and the notes just seem to disappear. One teacher has mailboxes for each child. A child delivers the mail in each box. At the end of the day, the kids are instructed to pick up their mail and put it in their school bag. Usually the notes get home, but there will be the child whose note you'll find at the end of the day sitting on the desk or in the mailbox. It happens. It's part of being a kid.

QUESTION:
But the note *has* to go home, how do I make sure it does get home?

ANSWER:
Another idea is to buddy up the kids. Have two kids be responsible for each other. One kid watches while the other child puts the note in the book bag and vice versa. Another solution is to have the buddies watch each other put it in their lunch box. Parents will see the note since lunches are made every day. Even after doing all of the suggestions, you'll still find notes on the floor.

QUESTION:
Then what, if I know the note *has* to go home?

ANSWER:
As a last resort, telephone home and explain to the parents what the contents of the note were. Also explain that their child is not being responsible and that's why you need to call home. Sometimes the child will take more responsibility, and sometimes they don't.

Documentation

Keeping precise educational records is an important part of teaching. You never know when you will be asked for information about a child.

QUESTION:

How important is the grade book I keep? How should I arrange the students?

ANSWER:

The grade book is very important . It is kept many years after the students have left and moved on to the next grade. The best way to keep track of grades is to put the students' names in alphabetical order. Don't write the student names in until a full week of school has gone by. The reason for this is you will probably have some additions during the week and, if filled in too early, your grade book will be out of order. I suggest you skip every other line when putting names in the book. When you have an addition later on in the year, you can print the child in without ruining your alphabetical order. Also, leave enough blank pages in between subjects for 40 weeks of grades. This is important, or you will be flipping pages when you are trying to save time. For example, after alphabetically writing in each child's name for math, skip about 4-5 pages before making the heading for social studies.

QUESTION:

Once I have written the names in, then what?

ANSWER:

Once the names are in, you will date every entry at the top of the grade book. At the bottom of the page, write the subject of the paper. For example, if you are grading two-digit addition with trading, you might want to indicate that at the bottom of your grade book. In doing so, during a conference, you can say ," Joey is having difficulty with addition of two-digit numbers." If you weren't specific enough, you'd have to say , "Joey is having difficulty with addition." The more specific you are, the better it is for everyone.

Sample Grade Book Entry			
MATH			
Student	Date 3/2/00		
Mary	86%		
Joe B.	95%		
Frank C.	89%		
+2digits			

Note that the date is at the top of the grade book and the assignment is at the bottom.

QUESTION:
How many grades per subject do I have to take? Do I have to put everything in my grade book?

ANSWER:
This is very specific to the school in which you teach. Some schools want one grade per week in every subject. Some schools want tests on one part of the grade book and weekly tests on another. You will need to check with other teachers in your building.

QUESTION:
After the ten week report card goes home, do I start again with new grades?

ANSWER:
Most schools start every 10 weeks with new grades. That is why you have perforations in the grade book. After you write the student names, leave enough pages for 40 weeks of grades per subject.

QUESTION:
How important is my planbook? I spend a lot of time writing everything down. Does anyone ever read it?

ANSWER:
My planbook is due once a week. I faithfully fill in the necessary spots. It keeps me focused. Planbooks are there for two reasons. One, in addition to the grade book, the planbook is kept for a period of time. Your planbook shows what you have taught throughout the year. It is also important to write in your plans that you have gone over fire drill and playground procedures. If anything ever happened to a student, you *must* show that you have gone over the rules of what to do in an emergency. Your planbook is a written document that not only shows what you have taught, but also serves as a tool for a substitute if you are sick. Having been a substitute teacher, I can tell you I have been saved by an accurate plan book and I have been frazzled by an incomplete planbook.

QUESTION:

How specific do I have to be in my planbook? Do I have to write everything out?

ANSWER:

No, it is not necessary. Generally if you are teaching a unit on the human heart your plans might look like this:

Sample Planbook Entry
Obj.)   To teach the students about the human heart and its purpose.
Procedure)   Students will look at the pictures and read pages 45–48 in their science book with a buddy. They will come up with reasons why the human heart is important. Students will discuss orally with class the reasons why the heart is important. Students will write these ideas in their science notebook.
MONDAY ─────────────────────────────► WEDNESDAY

Now, keep in mind that you may draw an arrow from Monday science to Wednesday science because this may take a few days.

Then on Thursday, for Science, you may show a movie about the human heart.

Thursday's plans would look like this:

Sample Planbook Entry #2
THURSDAY
Obj)   To review the purpose of the human heart.
Procedure)   Students will watch a video about the human heart and write down five important facts they learned about the heart to share with the class.

QUESTION:

I have a parent who is insisting that I never told her that her son wasn't passing the grade. I spoke with her several times on the phone, but she insists that I didn't. What can I do?

ANSWER:

Unfortunately, at this point, it is your word against her word. Did you *document* any of the telephone conversations? If you didn't, begin documenting now. A very simple way to document is to get index cards and a file folder. It's the same procedure I use for keeping track of words on a word ring which is mentioned in the Reading chapter on p. 101. It would be the same system, but a different purpose.

On the bottom of each index card, put the child's name. When you make a phone call, date the entry and the reason why you called. This is a very easy way to document what is going on for each student.

Some teachers keep a file folder on each child. That's important, but in addition I keep an index card on each child. The index cards have proven to be very useful when I have had a parent, teacher and administrator conference.

QUESTION:
Many of my children have divorced parents, do I need to send report cards home to both of them at separate addresses?

ANSWER:
Usually divorced parents will tell you how they want this handled. A good rule of thumb is to send home to *both* parents provided that there isn't a restraining order on either parent. If there is a restraining order, check with your administrator about how report cards should be handled.

QUESTION:
How important are cumulative folders? The principal at my school doesn't want the cumulative folder to leave the office.

ANSWER:
Cumulative folders, also known as Permanent Record folders, are important. They follow the child from Kindergarten through 12th grade. If you were to get a child in fourth grade that was having academic trouble, you could look back and see if it was noted in previous years. Reasons why academic assistance wasn't given should also be noted. Sometime parents do *not* want their child getting extra help if it means having the child leave the classroom. This must be documented.

QUESTION:
Why do I have to put test stickers on the permanent record card at the end of the year?

ANSWER:
Test stickers help the teacher know just where a student's strengths and weaknesses are. If you consistently notice a weakness in math, you might want to probe further to find out if this child has been given extra assistance in math. I know putting the stickers on are a nuisance, but they are a valuable tool in looking at the total child.

QUESTION:
Why do I have to put a final report card in the cumulative folder?

ANSWER:
The final report card has all the grades from the four marking periods. It helps to look at a child's progress throughout the year. You can quickly see what a child's strengths and weaknesses are by glancing at the report card. Previous teacher comments also help if you are particularly troubled by a student's progress.

QUESTION:
I received a very scathing note from a parent. Should this be put in the cumulative folder?

ANSWER:
That depends on what the note says. If the note is criticizing you as a teacher, I wouldn't put it in. If the note is commenting on the fact that you have not helped a child and you know you have, but there are other circumstances that are preventing this child from learning, I would put the note in. This problem is not going to go away and it is helpful for the next year's teacher to know what you have done to remediate the situation. *Most* parents are wonderful caring people. But you will get a few who will try to blame everyone else for the problem and not look at themselves. If this is the case, put the

note in, so the next teacher is aware that this problem already existed and the attempted solutions.

QUESTION:

I have a student who never returns notes that I have sent home. Do I need to document this?

ANSWER:

It depends on the reasons why you are sending the note home. Is it because the child is not doing well? If yes, you must document that you have sent this note home to the parents. A good rule of thumb is if the note is being sent home for an educational reason and you are getting no response from a parent, document this fact.

QUESTION:

But I really need to get in contact with this parent. What else can I do if the parent does not respond to my notes?

ANSWER:

You are assuming the note is getting home. Many children will "misplace" the note before it even gets home. You can use the reliable U.S. mail system. Those notes don't get lost. Always make a copy of what you send home and date everything. You think you will remember when you sent something home, but it is easier to just date everything that leaves your room.

QUESTION:

When there is a fire drill, am I responsible for anything other than the children?

ANSWER:

Yes, you need to bring your attendance book which will contain students names. If you get outside and count 25 heads, and you should have 26 heads, it is necessary to quickly figure out who is missing.

QUESTION:

How careful do I have to be with attendance everyday?

ANSWER:

You need to be very careful. Your attendance book is a legal document that is saved for a number of years. It can be bothersome to fill it in every day, but it's another necessary annoyance.

The Finals

Q & **A**   Top Ten No-No's

Just as there are things you should do as a beginning teacher, there are things you should not do. These are quick brief statements that will help you early on in your career. Please accept the statements as tools for guidance.

---

1. Do not begin the school year trying to be a "good friend" to the children. They have each other for friends. They need you to be their *teacher*. You will develop a special friendship with each child after you are secure in the role as teacher. Be their teacher first and friend second. My first year, I had it all backwards. I tried to be their friend first and teacher second. What a mistake that was.

2. Don't walk out of school empty handed. Most beginning teachers have so much school work to do, they get little sleep. If you don't have any school papers to correct on a particular night, carry out an empty brief case. People notice who takes work home with them.

3. Don't leave any personal belongings around for children to be tempted by. For example, purses, wallets, car keys, etc. should be locked in a cabinet.

4. Don't talk about children in the teachers' lunchroom. It's unprofessional and you never know who is related to the child you may be discussing. Talk about the weather, sports, hobbies, etc. Don't talk about a child.

5. Don't ever belittle children. If a child is being particularly disobedient, discuss the matter privately. You will have gained the respect of the disobedient child and the rest of the children in your class.

6. Don't ask children any personal questions. Allow them the privacy in their lives that you want in your life.

7. Try not to take your personal problems to school. When you shut your car door, leave all your problems in the car. Whatever may be upsetting you, talk to a colleague and get it off your chest before your school day begins. Some children come from chaotic homes and need a stable personality at school.

8. Don't give homework you haven't taught beforehand.

9. Don't forget what it's like to be a first year teacher. Share materials, ideas, and all of your knowledge with the next beginning teacher.

10. Don't give up on any child. Walk away if you need to, but always come back.

Final Word—
Top 10 Do's

There are some areas that don't fit into any specific category but are important. I have included them in this chapter titled Top Ten Do's.

1. Do ask questions. Just as you encourage your students to ask for help, I am encouraging you to ask colleagues for help too. There is no such thing as a dumb question. The question you don't ask could bring you trouble.

2. Do have all letters pre-approved by your administrator before sending them home to parents.

3. Do hang up students work using first names only. This way no one can compare children if only first names are used.

4. Do spend time in the teachers' faculty room for friendship and support. Teachers who have been teaching awhile can offer comfort and encouragement.

5. Do request for each child to bring in a box of tissue in the beginning of your school year. These boxes will be used throughout the year by all 25 noses.

6. Do keep a supply of paper plates, cups, napkins on hand for birthday treats. Many times cupcakes will come in, but no napkins. You'll have 25 chocolate fingers and faces.

7. Do subscribe to educational magazines. Usually your school library has a subscription you can read. Keep current.

8. Do buy holiday decorations after the holiday for the next year. You will save a lot of money buying this way.

9. Do keep units for science and social studies together in a box clearly marked for the specific subject area. Keep all experimental material in this box. It will save you time looking for a magnifying glass, etc. later.

10. Do enjoy your first year. It does get better and easier.

Q & A

Don't Give Up—
It Gets Easier

This letter is to all beginning teachers.

Dear Fellow Teacher,

This page seems to be the hardest to write. I know the expression, "been there . . . done that" is overworked, but I want you to know that I have been there . . . and done that. Teaching is very difficult. Don't let anyone tell you that is it easy to teach kids. You will look into their bright eyes and see the wonder they see. You will want to fill them with all the knowledge they are able to comprehend. You will go home weary over the fact that some children grow at their own pace and that pace doesn't seem quick enough for you. But I want you to know that it is all worth it. Once you have all your routines established, the school day will run smoother. Not only are you coming off summer vacation, but so are the kids. Give them time to adjust . Give yourself time to adjust.

If I had to choose something to do with the rest of my life, I would still choose teaching. I love it. Every day is a new challenge. Every day there is a new reward. Hang in there, it does get easier. Remember I've been there . . . done that, and I'm still teaching!

Games Appendix

As much as possible, I like to play games with children. Sometimes there is no educational purpose to the game. Sometimes there is a purpose. I have explained the game both ways: educational and non-educational.

QUESTION:
How do you play Mumball?

ANSWER:
Children of all ages enjoy this game. You need a soft sponge type ball. All children sit on their desks, chairs are pushed in. One child calls out the name of a fellow student. He throws the ball to this student. If the ball is caught, the child catching the ball stays in the game. If the child who is supposed to catch the ball misses, he's out. The game continues until one player is left. That's the winner of the game.

Educational Twist: Same procedure as above except when a child throws the ball, s/he not only calls out a student's name but also asks for a math fact. Let's suppose Frank throws a ball and says, "Mary, 3 x 5" Mary catches the ball and answers "15". What if Mary answers "8" and Frank doesn't realize it's the wrong answer? Both students are down. This prevents children from asking questions that are too difficult.

QUESTION:
How do you play Simon Says?

ANSWER:
All children are standing. One person is it. Let's call him Frank.

Frank	"Simon says do this." Frank extends his arms.
Children	All children extend their arms.
Frank	"Simon says do this". Frank puts his arms down.
Children	All children put their arms down.
Frank	"Do this." Puts one arm in the air.
Children	If anyone puts an arm in the air, s/he is out because the words "Simon Says" were *not* spoken.

Educational Twist:

Frank	"3 x 5 = 15" and extends arms to the side.
Children	All children extend arms to the side since 3 x 5 = 15
Frank	"4 + 8 x 0 = 0 puts arms down.
Children	All children put arms down since 4 + 8 x 0 = 0.
Frank	"8 + 5 = 14" puts one arm in the air.
Children	If anyone puts an arm in the air, s/he is out since 8 + 5 = 13.

If Frank asks a question he doesn't know the answer to, he is out. This prevents children from posing difficult probelms like "100 x 100 - 76 + 3"

QUESTION:
How do you play Four Corners?

ANSWER:
Label the corners in your room 1, 2, 3, and 4. One child, Frank, is it. He closes his eyes and slowly counts to 10 while the other children *walk* to a corner. While his eyes are closed, he calls out a number. Frank may say, "Corner Number 2". All children at corner number 2 have to sit down. Frank closes his eyes again and slowly counts to 10. Children once again move around the room. Frank calls out a number, "Corner number 4". The children at corner number 4 must sit down. The game continues until there is one person standing. If someone is *not* at a corner when Frank calls out a number, this person is also out. All children must be at a corner.

Educational Twist:
When Frank calls out a corner number, those children get to *stay* and they must answer some math flash card problems. If they answer correctly, they continue on with the game. If they answer incorrectly, they must sit down.

QUESTION:
What games can you play with a deck of cards?

ANSWER:
Two children can divide the deck in half. Have a calculator nearby. Each child flips over one card. Let's assume one child flipped over an 8 and another child flipped over a 6. The children can add the cards together. Whoever says the answer first keeps the cards. The winner is the person who has the most cards when both have exhausted their deck. The reason you have the calculator nearby is for a check if they don't know their math facts. Children can add the cards, subtract, multiply, or divide. You can take the face cards out, or keep them in the deck and have them count as 10 points.

QUESTION:
Any other games you can play with a deck of cards?

ANSWER:
Children can benefit from matching cards. Start out simple, take out 10 cards. Find a pair of 2's, 3's, 4's, 5's and 6's. Cards would be face down to begin with. Children would look for pairs. The game continues until all pairs have been matched. Once they have mastered 10 cards, increase it to 12 and so on.

Sample Matching Card Game Layout

Then child
flips over two
cards.

Since the 3s match, the child takes those two cards. The game continues.
The person who made the match gets another turn.

QUESTION:
Any spelling games?

ANSWER:
For this game, you will need three children. One child is the "teacher". The other children are playing a simple tic-tac-toe game. The board could look like this the following example.

Sample Tic-Tac-Toe Game Layout

Person A = X   Person B = O

Bonus

The teacher will ask a child to spell a word. If s/he spells the word correctly, s/he can put an "X" on the tic-tac-toe board. If a person selects "Bonus", that is a free point. The game continues until there is a winner. Children take turns being the teacher.

Reading and Writing References

The books listed below are just a suggested reading list. These are books I have in my professional library. All the books have to do with reading or writing.

Allington, R. & Walmsley, S. (1995). *No quick fix.* New York: Teachers College Press.

Avery, C. (1993). *And with a light touch: Learning about reading, writing and teaching with first graders.* Portsmouth, NH: Heinemann.

Clay, M. (1993). *An observation survey of early literacy achievement.* Portsmouth, NH: Heinemann.

Clay, M. (1993). *Reading recovery: A guidebook for teachers in training.* Portsmouth, NH: Heinemann.

Calkins, L. M. (1986). *The art of teaching writing.* Portsmouth, NH: Heinemann.

Cunningham, P. (1995). *Phonics they use.* New York: HarperCollins.

Frender, G. (1990). *Learning to learn.* Nashville, TN: Incentive Publications.

Harris, T. & Cooper, E. (1985). *Reading, thinking, and concept development.* New York: The College Board.

Hornsby, D., Sukarna, D., & Parry, J. (1986). *Read on: A conference approach to reading.* Sydney, Australia: Martin Educational.

McLaughlin, M. & Vogt, M. E. (1996). *Portfolios in teacher education.* Newark, DE: International Reading Association.

Parry, J. & Hornsby, D. (1985). *Write on : A conference approach to writing.* Melbourne, Australia: Nelson.

Parsons, L. (1990). *Response journals.* Portsmouth, NH: Heinemann.

Peterson R. & Eeds, M. (1990). *Grand conversations.* New York: Scholastic.

Routman, R. (1991). *Invitations: Changing as teachers and learners K–12.* Portsmouth, NH: Heinemann.

Trelease, Jim (1982). *The read-aloud handbook.* New York: Penguin.

Additional Suggested Readings

The following books are suggestions only. I do not own any of the books, but I spent time at the library looking over books that would be helpful to you as a beginning teacher.

Learning Styles

Association for Supervision and Curriculum Development. (1992). *Teaching to learning styles.* Alexandra, VA: Author.

Berman, S. (1995). *A multiple intelligence road to quality education.* Arlington Heights, IL: IRI/SkyLight Training and Publishing Inc.

Dunn, R. & Dunn, K. (1978). *Teaching students through their individual learning styles, a practical approach.* Reston, VA: Reston Publishing Company.

Fogarty, R. & Stoehr, J. (1995). *Integrating curricula with multiple intelligences.* Arlington Heights, IL: IRI Skylight.

Lazear, D. (1994). *Multiple intelligence approaches to assessment.* Tucson, AZ: Zephyr Press.

Lazear, D. (1991). *Seven ways of knowing: Teaching for multiple intelligences.* Arlington Heights, IL: IRI/SkyLight Training and Publishing Inc.

Lazear, D. (1994). *Seven pathways of learning, teaching students and parents about multiple intelligences.* Tucson, AZ: Zephyr Press.

McCarthy, B. (1987). *The 4 MAT system, teaching to learning styles with right/left mode Techniques.* Barrington, IL: Excel.

New York City School. (1994). *Multiple intelligences: Teaching for success.* St. Louis, MO: Hawthorne/Wolfe, Inc.

Silver, H. & Hanson, R. (1980). *Learning styles and strategies.* Moorestown, NJ: Hanson Silver and Associates Inc.

Behavior

Berman, S. (1997). *Making choice theory work in a quality classroom.* Arlington Heights, IL: IRI/SkyLight Training and Publishing, Inc.

Curwin, R. & Mendle, A. (1990). *Am I in trouble: Using discipline to teach young children responsibility.* Santa Cruz, CA: ETR Associates.

Curwin, R. & Mendle, A. (1998). *Discipline with dignity.* Alexandria, VA: Association for Supervision and Curriculum Development.

Kohn, A. (1993). *Punished by rewards.* New York: Houghton Mifflin Company.

Mendler, A. (1992). *What do I do when . . . ? How to achieve discipline with dignity in the Ccassroom.* Bloomington, IN: National Educational Service.

Porro, B. (1996). *Talk it out, conflict resolution in the elementary classroom.* Alexandria, VA: Association for Supervision and Curriculum Development.

Watson, G. (1998). *Classroom discipline problem solver.* West Nyack, NY: Center for Applied Research in Education.

Cooperative Learning

Kohn, A. (1986). *No contest, the case against competition.* New York : Houghton Mifflin Company.

Edited by Rolheiser, C. (1996). *Self evaluation: Helping students get better at it.* Ajax, Ontario: VisuTronX.

Index

Absent Notes, 152
Administrator 27, 29, 30, 94,139, 149
Allergies, 42, 60, 146
Annual Review, 72
Attendance, 157
Authors 105,106

Bathroom Routine, 13
Behavior 13, 29, 50, 59 73, 113, 117,
    131, 135, 138,140
Behavior Modification, 140
Behavior/Rules, 12
Birthday treats, 37
Board Meetings, 32
Board Members, 31
Books, 99, 100, 105
Bulletin Boards, 3
Bus, 4, 5 , 133, 134
Bus Driver, 42

CD Roms, 121
Child abuse, 29, 61
Children blood, 57
Children boundaries, 59
Children confidentiality, 56, 58,
Children death, 56
Children divorce, 57
Children favoritism, 57
Children ill, 56,57
Children Instructional Level, 82
Children Interests, 99
Children Medically fragile, 43
Children peers, 60, 61, 63
Children responsibility, 55
Children stealing, 63
Children unlikable, 57
Children Unpopular, 133
Committee Special Education (CSE),
    69,70
Computers, 121
Conferences, 38,39
Content, 14, 98, 101,102, 103, 143
Contract, 45, 47, 48
Copyright, 87
Correcting Papers, 88, 144

Counseling, 128
Cumulative Folder, 156
Custody, 134

D.E.A.R., 106
Discipline, 4, 137, 138
Divorce, 156
Documentation, 101

End of year, 24
Evaluation, 29, 30
Executive Session, 32

Field Trip, 33,115, 116,117, 118, 119
Fire Drill, 5, 11, 157
First Day, 7, 9, 10, 11, 55

Games, 11, 88, 111, 112, 113
Grade Book, 5
Grades, 91, 92, 108, 153, 154
Grievance, 46
Grouping, 95, 96, 98, 100

Holiday Celebrations, 33
Holiday Rules, 127
Homework, 101, 107, 108

Illness Procedures, 49
Inclusion Classroom, 70
Individualized Education Plan (IEP), 69,
    71
Internet Safety, 122
Internet Sites, 123, 124,

Learning Methods, 65, 66, 72, 113
Lice, 60
Lunch Procedures, 149, 150
Lying, 62

Maintenance, 41
Medicine, 43, 117
Newsletter, 40

Nurse, 43

Open House, 15, 17
Organization, 100, 101,
    121,132,133,134, 135, 136, 151,
    152

Parent, 9, 16, 20, 24, 28, 35, 36, 38, 41,
    59, 106, 108, 139, 144,151, 152,
    155, 157
Parent conferences, 39
Parents Custody, 10
Parents Field Trip, 116, 117, 118
Parents Helping Children, 125, 126, 127
Parent organization, 36
Percentile, 93
Permanent Record Card, 23, 156
Personality clash, 37
Phonics, 97, 100
Planbook, 5, 27, 154, 155
Plans, 50
Preparation Period, 149
Psychological Report, 70

Reading, 106
Recordkeeping, 122
Retention, 24, 28, 29, 36, 37
Rules, 12, 50, 60, 131, 137

Safety, 145, 146, 147
School Rules, 5
Search Engine, 123
Seating Arrangements, 3, 4,
Secretary, 41
Self-Contained Classroom, 70
Sloppy copy, 84, 85
Special Education Identification, 73
Special Education Teacher, 71
Spelling, 78, 79, 80
Standardized Testing, 21
Standardized Tests, 93
Standards, 21, 22,
Stanine, 93
State Guidelines, 6
Stealing, 138
Subject Expectation, 21, 22
Substitute, 49, 50, 51
Substitute folder, 49
Substitute Plans, 51
Supplies, 4, 14, 87, 109
Syllables, 80

Teacher Aide, 42, 151
Tenure, 47

Tenure/renewable, 46
Test, 91, 93
Time Management, 19, 20, 21,143, 144
Triennial, 70
Trust, 137

Union, 45, 46

Videos, 7
Vowels, 81, 82

Word Recognition, 82
Worksheet alternatives, 87, 88, 89
Worksheet, 98
Writing, 77, 78, 79, 83, 84, 85, 86, 119
Writing Computers, 122

Joanna Montagna Torreano

EDUCATION RESOURCE CENTER
UNIVERSITY OF DELAWARE